Mind Control 101

How to Influence the Thoughts and Actions of Others Without Them Knowing or Caring

by

Dantalion Jones

Mind Control Publishing
First published 2006
ISBN: 978-1-4303-1815-6

Copyright © Dantalion Jones 2011
2nd Edition

All rights reserved. Without limiting the rights under copyrights reserved above, no part of this publication may be reproduced, stored in or introduced into a retrieval system, or transmitted, in any form or by any means (electronic, mechanical, photocopying, recording or otherwise), without the prior written permission of the copyright owner.

Dedication

To my faithful djinn, familiar and constant companion, Dantalion, the 71st spirit of the Goetia, "His Office is to teach all Arts and Sciences unto any; and to declare the Secret Counsel of any one; for he knoweth the Thoughts of all Men and Women, and can change them at his Will. He can cause Love, and show the Similitude of any person, and show the same by a Vision, let them be in what part of the World they Will."

Also to Robert Greene who read over 1,000 books for me so that I might learn to spiritualize everything and treat life like a glorious campaign.

Table Of Contents

Introduction 1

PART 1
What is Mind Control? 2
Introduction to Mind Control 6
Where is Mind Control Used? 9
Models of Mind Control 10
A Brief History of Mind Control 14
Memes and Mind Control 20
Only Idiots are Influenced by Mind Control? 23
So You Want to Learn to Use Mind Control? 24
What are the Related Fields of Mind Control? 28

PART 2
The Techniques of Mind Control 32
Behavioral Conditioning 34
Coercion 37
Social Pressure & Mob Mind Control 40
Social Influence a la Robert Cialdini 43
NLP - Neuro Linguistic Programming 47
Meta Programs 61
Forbidden Dark Patterns 71
Hypnosis 84
Psychic Cold Readings 88
Dumb Blonde Mind Control 98
Appealing to Basic Human Responses 99
Interviews & Interrogation 104
Gaslighting Old & New 125
Pharmacological Mind Control 131
The Power & Use of Symbols & Rituals for Mind Control 140
Psychic Influence 141
Other Techniques of Mind Control 146
Cult Mind Control Tactics & Strategies 152
The 5 Steps of Mind Control Outlined by Edgar H. Schein 158
How to Create a Recovered Memory 159
Mind Tricks with Others 161
Enchantment 170
What are the Personal Dangers of Using Mind Control? 171
Conclusion 174
Recommended Mind Control Movies 175
Additional Resources 176

Mind Control 101

Introduction

Why in the world would someone write a book on Mind Control?

More specifically, why would someone write a book on how to use Mind Control, as though it is a great and wonderful thing to "fuck with peoples heads?"

The answer is that, as much as we try to elevate ourselves above being human animals, we are, in fact, animals. We are subject to the wants and desires of any being with a genetic make up and vertebrae. To rise above that is an admirable aspiration and one that I encourage anyone to take on as a worthy spiritual endeavor.

But to deny that we are, truly, animals is to lie to ourselves. We must interact in a social environment and deal with people who may not be so enlightened and spiritually advanced as we are. They may desire what we have and be secretly filled with envy and contempt. The worst event is to have these suspicions fulfilled and then be pulled down into the politics of man.

In this event, what are the options? Do we deny that it is happening and hope others will be touched by our honesty and good will enough to change? Or do we drop our highest spiritual ideals and play their game?

I would like to suggest a radically different strategy. Take the game of manipulation and Mind Control and make it a part of your spirituality.

By doing so, we neither deny manipulation and Mind Control, nor do we surrender to it. Instead we embrace it and see it for what it is - a tool for our growth.

What I describe is the spiritual life of the warrior, who embraces life and sees every battle as an expression of life, not death. To this warrior, every moment is a chance to live fully and aspire, while walking in the world yet guided by something higher.

If you are so bold and fearless to embrace Mind Control in this manner, every interaction is lifted above the mundane and worldly and becomes a vehicle for your spirituality. You will be lifted and remain untouched, even amid the most vulgar of human politics. Your war will be your temple.

You should be warned. As you read this, there is nothing that will be withheld. Like the warrior, there are many unpleasant things that you must learn about this life you choose. While you are obligated to learn these secrets, you are not obligated to use them.

I bid you to walk fearlessly. Face your demons and laugh at them. Make them your servants and walk untouched.

PART I:
What is Mind Control?

Mind Control. When you hear those words, a myriad of images may come to mind. You might envision a devious man, using the power of his mind and will to dominate the actions of some unsuspecting and innocent women.

You may think of some clandestine cabal of world leaders, secretively planning the next steps toward a unified world economy.

Or perhaps you are the cult leader (one of my favorite images), with a gathering of loyal followers, ready to hear every word.

It is not likely you have in mind a loving parent reading to his children or an Alcoholics Anonymous meeting helping its members live a decent life of sobriety.

It is also unlikely that, as you stand in your favorite church of worship, you will recognize the grasp that Mind Control has on you.

Or as you sit with your psychiatrist, you are unlikely to be aware of the subtle acts of Mind Control that are being used on you.

But it is there.

And for the sake of this book, any attempt to bring about a change in your thoughts and feelings, and therefore your actions, is an act of Mind Control.

That may sound shocking, because most people see Mind Control as a bad thing done by bad people. So let me make it clear - the intention and motives of the controller are not relevant to this discussion. The controller may be motivated by the most altruistic ideals or may only want your money.

This book will attempt to uncover the methods of how those thoughts and feelings are instilled to bring about the controller's outcome.

To make a distinction, Mind Control differs from the vulgar actions and tactics of coercion. Coercion is when all a controller wants is to have someone make a specific action and has no concern

Mind Control 101

for their motivation. Threats, guilt and humiliation will usually do the job. But coercion lacks any form of grace or elegance.

Coercion cares nothing about the thoughts and feelings of the people being coerced. This is the major difference between coercion and Mind Control.

Because many so-called cults use coercion to get compliance from their subjects, the topic will be discussed, but it is the goal of this book to aspire to something higher, namely Mind Control. In the next chapter of this book the various models of Mind Control will be covered.

The difference between Mind Control and persuasion is subtle, but nonetheless important. Consider all power of one form or another as a hierarchy. By moving up each level one controls more and more power. Persuasion starts at the bottom, while Mind Control seeks to control the top of the pyramid. As an example, persuasion seeks to sell a widget and overcome the buyer's tendency to say "I have to ask my wife." Mind Control, on the other hand, seeks to make the thought of not owning the widget blasphemous and unnatural.

It is a good idea to remember that true Mind Control is difficult and unnatural, because it requires the controller to think above the present short-term and think beyond mere appearances. The majority of the world responds to what they see and reacts to it by thinking in terms of the tactics that will get them what they want. Mind Control, true quality Mind Control, requires thinking in terms of strategy. Thinking far enough ahead, so that your real desire is hidden, yet your outcome is still achieved.

No simple task.

It requires knowing how people think and respond and a knowledge of the individual's personal impulses and weaknesses.

More importantly, it requires knowing yourself and being able to control your impulses to react. Your goals, your highest ambitions, must be held secret and every action measured by how close it brings you to your goal.

One way of distinguishing how people think is in terms of *serial*, *linear* and *non-linear* thinking.

Serial thinking is the act of thinking and responding in an

automatic fashion. Serial thinking is a result of our evolution and is quite useful. By simply reacting to the situation at the moment, it prevents us from having to think too much. It is also how sheep are led to slaughter.

Linear thinking is a step up and requires forethought and the ability to predict, in some way, the consequences of actions and various paths that lead to our goals and desires. For the average chess player, the game is an excellent example of how to stretch linear thinking to its limits.

Non-linear thinking does not stop at the chess board. At its pentacle, it incorporates all dimensions of space and time. While a linear thinking chess player may aim to win each game and become a world champion, the non-linear player will be able to see how losing a game will position them to play an opponent that will be easier to beat and therefore give themselves and the game greater publicity. A non-linear thinking player may even see so far ahead, knowing their own limitations and the limitations of the game, that at one point, they will stage a huge outburst, promising to never play the game again and garner exposure for one of their other ambitious projects.

The art of Mind Control is more than just responding to the situation (serial thinking) or having a structured plan to get your outcome (linear thinking). It is the ability to be fluid, when responding to a fluid environment. You must know your goal; you must know yourself; you must know your environment; and you must know the people you influence, in every way possible. And you must do it all while outwardly appearing to be like everyone else around you.

This is no easy task - but it is worthy of your efforts.

To aspire to this ideal promises that, at every turn, you will learn something about yourself and your world.

Of course, if you are interested in Mind Control, it is probably a good idea to discuss the ethics of Mind Control. I'm not one to preach morality, and nowhere in this book will you read how you should use Mind Control.

This is not a book on ethics, and you can guess that there are plenty of people and organizations who have used this technology,

Mind Control 101

with no concern about how it affects people. I know plenty of men who have used Mind Control to get laid. It is truly not that hard. The ones who are good at it can frame their actions, so that the women involved understand that it is a way to give them the pleasure they will enjoy. In other words, they appreciate the effort made to seduce them. Others are not so skilled and would do better to remain silent about their actions and intentions.

Let me, therefore, recommend that you use what you learn here, as if it were to be used on you.

So, if you aren't annoyed with Mind Control being used on you (believe me, it is being used on you all the time), and you are generally a happy person, then it is probably okay to do the same with others.

As a general rule, if you decide to use Mind Control, and you are motivated by anger or hurt, it is very likely that you will hurt people in the process. Perhaps that's not a concern for you. So be it. However, you should be warned never to underestimate people's desire to get even, and change your actions accordingly.

As a final note, through all of this, you may find it so enlightening that you feel it is worth sharing, especially with people close to you. One might believe that others will appreciate being awoken from their ignorance.

I dare you to try.

What you will find is that sleep (metaphoric sleep) is the natural state of the mind. People will equate your efforts to awaken them with an attempt to change them. While people might not mind changing, they resist being changed. Therefore, it is best to keep your own counsel.

Do people need waking up? Of course, but let them do it in their own time. Until then, it will be you and I who benefit from these insights.

The movie The Matrix offers an analogy. In the movie, humanity was subjugated, through Mind Control, to serve a machine. Supposing that you are an insignificant power source, subordinate to a huge world dominating machine - would you have swallowed the red pill, as the main character, Neo did, in order to be 'woken up' and realize it?

Mind Control 101

"We live on a placid island of ignorance in the midst of black seas of infinity, and it was not meant that we should voyage far."
-H.P. Lovecraft

The Intended Audience

This book was written to appeal to a wide range of people, who can apply its knowledge in the area of human interaction.

Your ambitions may vary as much as your interests; whether you seek world domination or to merely better your interpersonal communications, this book will have something for you.

It is safe to say that the only person who will not benefit from applying this knowledge is the individual isolated from all human contact.

There have been many people who have preceded you, and you and anyone else can learn from them. You can study them, or use them as models of behavior. Who are these people? Martin Luther King Jr., Golda Meir, Fidel Castro, Alfred Hitchcock, Nepoleon Bonaparte, Salvidor Dali, Alexander the Great, Indira Gandhi, Anton Szandor LaVey, Marlon Brando, John Wayne, Darth Vader, Don Vito Corleone and King Lear.

Welcome to the brotherhood.

Introduction to Mind Control

To understand the process of Mind Control, it is necessary to have a basic understanding of the human mind.

People make decisions on every level, in a way that is unique to each of them. Those decisions are based on mental filters that are used to perceive the self and its environment. These filters are best understood in the form of questions that people ask themselves. Keep in mind that these questions are asked unconsciously, therefore people are unaware of them, but they can be deduced by a person's behaviors and the way they react to events.

These questions are not the same in every context. A person may make major decisions about relationships based on the question, "Would this person provide me with security?" But in the context of buying a car, the question might be, "Will it get me attention?" or vice versa.

These questions may be numerous and have a hierarchy of

priority. For example, determining whether to consider someone as a sexual partner may involve having to fulfill the following questions.

"Am I attracted to their appearance?" "Do I feel safe with this person?" "Can I see myself having sex with this person?" "Can I see myself having sex with this person more than once?" "Will I feel good about myself, if I have sex with this person?" and so on.

People will respond differently to the same situations, depending on the questions (filters) they ask. One person facing the loss of a job may ask, "What did I do wrong?" in which case they notice, find or create what they did wrong. Another person in the same situation may ask, unconsciously, "How is this an opportunity for me?" and see the same situation as an opportunity.

Much to the amazement and amusement of many rational thinkers, there is no end of people, who habitually focus on the problems, rather than the solutions to the things life throws at them.

Of course, none of these questions are asked on a conscious level. Many of these questions/filters are so deeply ingrained, that it may offend people, if they are asked to consider the situation in any other possible way.

The degree to which you can direct a person's filters and the unconscious questions they ask themselves is the degree to which you can direct their thoughts and actions. In other words, Mind Control. This holds true of the questions you ask yourself, as well.

So, understanding this, you can start your journey of learning Mind Control, by examining your own filters/questions that lead you to make decisions and, at the same time, observe the people around you, as well.

A couple of filters/questions you could add to your own personal repertoire, for the purpose of learning Mind Control is, "What can I assume is true of this person, that's not overtly apparent?" and "How can I direct their attention, in order to get my outcome?"

You will be surprised how much you learn.

Mind Control goes by many names: persuasion, seduction, manipulation, sales skills, politics, advertising, and so on. The one thing that they all have in common is the desire to change people's minds and behaviors.

Now, I ask you, is this common?

Mind Control 101

You bet it is. In fact, it is one of the main functions of communication. Yes, even when you are talking to yourself (absent of any mental disorder), the reason you do it is to direct your thoughts, actions and behaviors.

The ugly truth is we use Mind Control every time we open our mouths to talk. While those two words "Mind Control" may have a grating ring to most of our ears, it doesn't prevent it from being a fact of everyday life. Many people will violently deny that they use it.

The more we try to deny how we use Mind Control, the more ineffective we are at it.

It is time to raise the phrase "Mind Control" from its improperly placed gutter, and hold it up to examination as a simple fact of human nature. That means being truly honest about ourselves, while keeping our intentions close to the vest.

Some might argue that honesty is the best policy.

As much as that is the ideal, and few people will eagerly tell you otherwise, the opposite is usually true.

I was in a conversation with a close friend, who expressed to me that, as much as he likes and admires me, he was concerned about my tendency to withhold and obfuscate information, telling me it seemed to him to be the main obstacle to what he considers my success.

There is no doubt that he believes what he says and that his intentions are well-meaning, but reality teaches a different lesson.

To prove it, all one has to do is be completely honest about your intentions, whenever you go on a first date. Perhaps you have visions of matrimony in mind with your date. Or perhaps your only goal is to lead your date into an unrestrained expression of sexual debauchery. Either way, it is very unlikely that you will achieve your goals, by openly stating your intent from the start.

Truth, it seems, is a caustic and volatile chemical, when added to most human interactions. When it is administered without restraint, the only certain outcome is that the outcome will be uncertain. Thankfully, Truth is also very malleable and relatively safe, when cautiously administered in deluded forms.

It is best, then, to be judicious with your expressions of true intentions and feelings, until a reliable response can be determined.

In the meantime, we can look for evidence of how pervasive Mind Control is in our daily lives.

"Judge a man by his questions rather than his answers."
~ Voltaire

Where is Mind Control Used?

Everywhere!

Here is a list of how Mind Control is used in everyday life:

* Motivating a child to eagerly perform better in school
* Creating obedience to a religious of political figure
* Creating a feeling of superiority towards one group
* Motivating a prospect to buy a specific product or service
* Creating panic to sell a certain stock
* Instilling trust in the authority that is speaking to you on the television
* Creating contempt for the competition while establishing greater customer loyalty
* Bringing in greater revenues
* Bringing an attractive person into a romantic or sexual encounter
* Selling an undervalued product for a higher price
* Talking a cop out of a traffic ticket
* Making a spectator believe in psych abilities
* Causing someone to reevaluate their prior beliefs

The list can go on and on.

In all of these cases, the controller clearly knows his or her outcomes and objectives.

It is safe to say that any time you want something that involves motivating someone to do something, or when people do something without questioning why they are doing it, some form of Mind Control is involved, whether it is intentional or not. So we are using Mind Control all the time. Even the act of having your partner take out the garbage could not happen, without some form of setup, conditioning and Mind Control. If you doubt it, ask a stranger to take out your garbage, and see what kind of compliance you get.

As you will learn, Mind Control requires thinking on a higher level than the subject and veiling the strings of control with the everyday distractions of daily life. As one seeks to control the higher levels of a hierarchy of power, something interesting occurs. The visibility of the control becomes less obvious to the subject(s), as they become more involved with their day-to-day concerns.

Mind Control is everywhere. Once you realize the depth of Mind Control in your life, your only option, outside of paranoia, is a calm, almost Buddha-like all-knowingness, that recognizes the ubiquitous presence of Mind Control, and to set out to use it to your advantage. While this mindset can be encouraged, no one can teach it. Only through patience, effort and a little suffering can you gain this invaluable perspective.

Models of Mind Control

If Mind Control is about controlling the thoughts, emotions and actions of others, there are several functional models that will help you do that.

To find out just how Mind Control creates the degree of compliance that one wants, let's consider some common models of Mind Control.

Behavioral Modification/Conditioning Model

As with every case of Mind Control, the controller knows what he wants people to do and wants them to do it willingly and for, what they think, are their own reasons.

The Behavioral Modification/Conditioning Model works by a system of stimuli, in the form of rewards and punishments, based on the behaviors of the subject. So in much the same way as you would train a dog to do tricks, you can train a person to willingly take part in some action.

Behavioral Modification/Conditioning requires a series of steps that rewards good behavior and punishes bad behavior. But let's say you want your subject to steal some candy from a store (or worse). Using the behavioral modification model, you would first reward them for "thinking creatively" outside the norm of social ethical behavior. After they have become used to thinking out side the norm, and you reward them at every turn for it, it is time to move to the next level. At this next stage, rewards are given for taking actions outside the norm but sanctioned within a social structure or group.

Mind Control 101

College hazing is a good example. Each act the subjects perform that is outside the norm (but protected within the group) is rewarded, perhaps with a slap on the back or toast in their name.

With the proper conditioning, at the final stage, the subjects are then told to go steal some candy. And when this is completed, a rousing party is held in their honor.

It wouldn't take much more than several of these exercises, to have them do something even more malicious.

A punishment when an action is not taken could be something as mild as having members of the group scoff in disdain. They will also be given a choice to deal with the consequences of not acting as requested. This creates the illusion of free will.

To use the Behavioral Modification/Conditioning model skillfully and with stealth, the controller must make the rewards huge and the punishments mild but memorable. This will prevent the subject from believing they were coerced in any way.

Scientology has a very thorough behavioral conditioning process that they refer to as "The Training Routines" or "TRs," The TRs are presented as a communication training at the very beginning of someone's interest in Scientology. The TRs are a progressive set of exercises that lead the subject to instantly respond to a command that is given in what is called a 'tone 40' voice. Once the subject learns to respond as asked in this way, they can be easily told to take out their check book and enroll in the next training.

Hardwired Model

In much the same way that a doctor may tap your knee, and it reflexes with a jerk of the leg, so too are there certain ways that we as humans are hardwired to respond. While this will be covered in more detail in the section entitled, Appealing to Basic Human Responses, two examples of this are The Need to Be Special and The Scapegoat.

An example of The Need to Be Special is in telling a subject that they are uniquely qualified for a task and appreciated for their skills and knowledge. The hardwired human response to this is one of agreement and a feeling of satisfaction.

The Scapegoat is the basic human need to know that our problems are not our fault, even if, in fact, they are.

Mind Control 101

There is a great deal of talk among the Human Potential Movement to "take responsibility for your life," and on a conscious level, it makes complete sense. If we look at our life as something that we are in complete control of, we feel more empowered, will tend to act more decisively and be happier people, simply because we choose it. Nonetheless, the world has other plans and will often throw us a curve-ball that we didn't expect; people we trust will rip us off; we'll deal with bills and financial concerns; and loving relationships will end. In all of these cases, it is still a relief to know that "it is not our fault." We will gladly take sides with strangers, who will support us throwing stones at our enemies.

I was discussing this with a friend, who eagerly agrees with the concept of 'complete personal responsibility.' When the topic turned to a problem he was having with a client, I responded by lambasting the client ,expressing how it was all the client's fault and that my friend was not responsible for the troubles. He was instantly appeased and showed his appreciation at my concern. I then told to him how I was using The Scapegoat on him, and he immediately understood its power.

The Need to Be Special and The Scapegoat are just two of the examples that show how we are hardwired to respond.

NLP Model

NLP stands for Neuro Linguistic Programming. It is field of study that was developed in the late 70s by two scientists, Richard Bandler and John Grinder.

They wanted to discover why certain therapists could deal with their clients and get very rapid results, where other therapists seem to take months and years.

In doing this, they discovered that there are certain mental processes we all go through, to make decisions and to make changes. If someone (anyone) knows another's process for making changes, they just have to conform to that process, and change will occur.

It is essentially having the road map to someone's mind. With it, you can guide the person to do a whole myriad of things, without them even knowing what you are doing. As a result, many people have applied NLP to sales and persuasion, while others have applied it to seductions.

Mind Control 101

What makes NLP unique as a model of Mind Control is that it treats people as distinct individuals, not as a mass of hardwired robots. This means that each person has their own processes for change and these processes are unique to them.

The central key in using NLP as a Mind Control tool is to find ways to elicit people's individual processes. These processes can be in the form of beliefs, personal assumptions, tendencies and values, as well as their strategy for making decisions. Once you discover an individual's unique processes, the doors are wide open for Mind Control.

Environmental Control Model

The Environmental Control Model can be a lot of fun and a lot of work.

It requires that the controller take into account everything that the subject will experience, so that they will naturally conclude exactly what the controller wants and, as a result, fulfill the controller's objective, without considering any other possibility or option.

It truly requires seeing a much bigger picture of what is happening.

Think of how magicians control the environment, to have you believe the effect. A good magician won't tell you, "This is an ordinary deck of playing cards." Instead, he will fan them for you and even have you handle them, so that you conclude, on your own, what he wants you to believe. All the while, the deck could marked, rigged or be a prop of one sort or another.

To use the Environmental Mind Control model, consider this phrase, "No can resist what they can't detect."

The Environmental Control Model is also a favorite of con-men. If you are in a hospital parking lot, and you see a man in a white coat, with a stethoscope dangling out of his pocket, a name tag that says "Samuel Wallis, MD., Urology," who asks for jumper cables to start his car, you naturally assume he is a doctor. More importantly, you don't assume he is not a doctor.

The pentacle of the Environmental Control Model is the movie, "The Matrix."

For the people who lived connected to the Matrix, everything was just as they thought it was, with the worries and desires of everyday life. All the while, they were protected from discovering that they were nothing more than AA Batteries, used to power a global machine.

To use the Environmental Mind Control model effectively, you must first ask what you want your subject to do and what to believe, and then create the environment that will naturally make them conclude what you want. Doing this on a large scale can prove difficult, because of the numerous variables one must control. On a smaller scale, however, it can be quite simple.

Take the example of going to a religious retreat. The participants are isolated from the rest of the world. No TV or newspaper. No cell phones or computers. They are then asked to remove their shoes and be silent when in certain locations, as a sign of reverence. After doing this for a period of time, it does not take much for them to begin to believe what they are told to believe.

A con-man will also use isolation by making sure his mark is constantly occupied by his con-man collaborators, whose jobs are to make certain that the mark's attention is continually directed exactly where they want it.

These are merely models of Mind Control, not the techniques and tactics. As models, they provide hints at the possible strategies that make Mind Control possible.

The next chapter will cover how Mind Control, techniques and tactics, have been used on a historical basis.

A Brief History of Mind Control

Mind Control is not bad, in itself; it is a process that has evolved as a survival mechanism for the group. In other words, if the group could stay together in an effective way, they would have a better chance of collectively surviving what the world throws at them. If one person didn't conform in thought and behavior to the group norm, they could threaten the groups survival. They further learned that, by influencing others outside of the clan in certain ways, they could prevent attacks.

Keep in mind that, while most of us value and tout the virtues of freedom and personal independence, these are new concepts when compared to the long span of human history. Mind Control has been the rule, not the exception.

Parents and upbringing

Beliefs are born from our experiences and not from facts. In fact a belief is a belief because it is not a fact. Facts can be proven but beliefs must be argued.

However, most people do not make these distinctions and hold their beliefs as facts, stating them without even the consideration of anything contrary.

Parents are no exception. Thus parents unknowingly take part in the most thorough Mind Control processes that are available, by controlling every aspect of a child's life (Environmental Control Model). They reward preferred behavior and punish the bad (Behavioral Modification Model). Some who are good at parenting understand a child's unique tendencies and dispositions and controls them by accommodating this uniqueness (NLP Model).

Teaching Institutions

The worlds second oldest profession is, in fact, a well crafted Mind Control experiment. There are many features and techniques of Mind Control at work in any classroom. The most obvious is peer pressure, designed to enforce conformity.

Other techniques include Behavioral Modification of rewards and punishments that work together, with the intention that everyone learn the same information. The result, and perhaps the hidden intention, is to instill conformity of thought and behavior, as the rule. A possible secondary hidden intention is to forbid free thought and creativity. Yes, modern pedagogy, regardless of its intentions, uses tried and tested Mind Control methods, as a matter of course.

Religion and the Application of Mind Control

This is one of my favorite topics, because religious organizations use every Mind Control method available.

Let's focus on the stated and unstated intentions of most religious groups and how they use the means of Mind Control to reach their ends.

Their stated intention is to get closer, as individuals, to their god. In doing so, a devout follower will eagerly apply any Mind Control method on themselves. This might even include the various deprivations that would normally fall under the category of self-imposed coercion.

The unstated aims of religious Mind Control are many, among them are to:
* Raise money for the church or church leaders.
* Instill fear of disobeying church doctrine.
* Create a sense of moral superiority to the devout.
* Create contempt for the non-believers.
* Unify the group to work together.
* Recruit non-believers into the flock.

Anton Mesmer

Anton Mesmer is the founder of mesmerism and the forerunner of hypnosis.

Mesmer believed that all living organisms have a magnetic fluid running through them and that, by making passes over the body with magnets, one can control the flow of that fluid and alter the person's health and mental state.

Later in his career, he found that making these passes without magnets created the same result.

What he fell upon was the wonderful phenomenon of human suggestibility. By speaking with confident authority and telling people what they would experience, people experienced just that. By adding the effect of rituals, it was made even more compelling. People would swoon and fall over under his control.

MKULTRA

Project MKULTRA (also known as MK-ULTRA) was the code name for a CIA mind-control research program that began in the 1950s and continued until the late 1960s. There is much published evidence that the project involved, not only the use of drugs to manipulate persons, but also the use of electronic signals to alter brain functioning.

It was first brought to wide public attention by the U. S. Congress (in the form of the Church Committee), a presidential commission (known as the Rockefeller Commission) and also to the U. S. Senate.

On the Senate floor, Senator Ted Kennedy said:

"The Deputy Director of the CIA revealed that over 30

universities and institutions were involved in an 'extensive testing and experimentation' program, which included covert drug tests on unwitting citizens 'at all social levels, high and low, native Americans and foreign.' Several of these tests involved the administration of LSD to 'unwitting subjects in social situations.' At least one death, that of Dr. Olson, resulted from these activities. The Agency itself acknowledged that these tests made little scientific sense. The agents doing the monitoring were not qualified scientific observers."

MKULTRA did experiments in every conceivable area of Mind Control, from the coercive to the covert, in an attempt to find out how to control the thoughts and actions of groups and individuals.

Keep in mind that this was during the time of the Cold War, when many felt that the government was being assailed from every direction.

By doing just a little searching on the Internet, anyone can find government documents that describe the depth of sincere interest the U. S. government had in Mind Control. It is safe to assume that these now public documents represent only a portion of what the government does in the name of national security and that some other experiments are yet unrevealed and still ongoing.

L. Ron Hubbard

There are plenty of people who have started cults and religious movements that could be mentioned here, but L. Ron Hubbard stands out as an icon for his creative use of Mind Control.

Hubbard is best known as a science fiction writer and founder of Scientology. He is quoted as prophetically saying, "If you want to make a lot of money, start your own religion." And he did just that.

Hubbard invented a process he called Dianetics, which he proposed was able to clear people of all their worldly and spiritual problems and had the potential to give them super powers of perception and influence.

Through his church, Scientology, members would go through lengthy and expensive trainings called 'auditing,' to remove 'engrams' from their nervous system, that they claimed to be the origin of all human problems.

Being a creative and prolific writer, Hubbard and his followers created a complex and compelling process that would lead its members into a video game-like world view, in which they would zap hindering engrams and release 'Operating Thetans' from the psyche, so that each person could be free to fulfill their true potential.

Clearly Hubbard was a creative genius, who used his love of science fiction to compel people into his Scientology/Dianetics Mind Control system.

Robert Cialdini and Social Influence

In 1984, Robert Cialdini wrote a landmark book called Influence: *How and Why People Agree to Things,* in which he describes six very basic principles of social interaction, in which people consistently respond.

Advertising

It is no secret that the advertising industry's goal is to manipulate people to buy, buy and buy more of whatever they are peddling.

Suffice to say that they use every tool of Mind Control that is known to man, from social pressure to NLP to subliminal suggestions.

Because money is the motivator, they pull out all the stops and test every ad, to get the maximum effect.

Landmark Forum

Landmark Forum is a form of self-improvement training that originated in the 1970s, with 'est' or Erhart Seminar Training. People would go through weekend and week-long training sessions, and emerge laughing and smiling, trying fervently to enroll their friends.

There is a wonderful paradox with Landmark Forum. It has an overt intention to liberate people from all previous forms of Mind Control, so that they will take responsibility for themselves and think independently. The irony is the incredible depth of Mind Control that is used to accomplish their end.

In the early days of 'est,' participants would be locked in a room with restricted bathroom breaks, told to remove their watches because, "Now is the only time you need." They would endure coercive berating from the seminar leaders and volunteers (called facilitators), who had already gone through the training. Eventually, the participants would break down and yield, as in traditional brainwashing programs, to accept what was being said as true.

They were then given the final blow. They were told that none of what they have gone through had any meaning at all, except for what they gave it. They were told that they are the ONLY one who was responsible for what they had experienced, and for their life in general, and all the blaming and scapegoating was bullshit. In those early days of "est," every overt coercive brainwashing method was used, leading up to the final revelation. The effect was astounding.

Since then. "est" has transformed its name and image to Landmark Forum, and they have managed to add a bit more of the velvet glove to their steel-hammered approach.

The irony of the "est" and Landmark Forum training is the way in which they would coercively steal the control from people, so that they would fully accept it back, when offered.

Charles Manson and Other Modern Mind Control Strangeness

Charles Manson was a small-time crook, who spent most of his life in prison, until his release in the 1960s. In his 30s, and living in the heart of the hippie movement in California, Manson discovered two things that he exploited to his advantage. First, the anti-establishment movement, that encouraged people to enter a world of self-exploration, to "Turn on, tune in and drop out." The second was the prevalence of the mind-altering drug LSD.

Manson combined them in the form of sex orgies that propelled people far beyond their normal acceptable behaviors, in the name of freeing themselves. But Manson's personal psychosis and delusions took charge, when he ultimately told his followers to commit acts of murder, to incite a war between the races.

What makes Manson unique as a study of Mind Control was that he was the first documented case that combined the use of modern psychoactive drugs and sex, to instill new beliefs and behaviors in his subjects.

Other Modern Strangeness

There are a lot of things that are best categorized as "fringe" topics of Mind Control. Among these are radionics, remote viewing and psychic influence.

These fields have a format but tend to lack the ability to

objectively quantify results. Results are reported, but they are often sporadic and subjective in nature.

An Exercise for Your Benefit

If true Mind Control is being used on you at every turn, it provides you with a wonderful opportunity to examine it. Start to examine the more obvious efforts of others to influence you. It will be in conversation, images, emails, advertising, TV shows, music and more. Ask yourself what their real intent could be. You will find that there are many possible answers, because, if it is true Mind Control, the intent is often veiled behind a glossy image.

More importantly, examine how you respond to these things. It could be exactly the very response that the controllers wanted. If that is true, and you are responding just as they wanted, ask yourself what tools they used to do it and how they were able to mask their intent. Always keep in mind that the intent you judge them to have may just be exactly what they want to you believe.

Memes and Mind Control

The term 'meme' was coined in 1976 by Richard Dawkins.

It refers to a replicator of cultural information that one's mind transmits (verbally or by demonstration) to another mind. Dawkin's examples of memes are tunes, catch-phrases, clothes fashions, ways of making pots or of building arches. Other examples include deities, concepts, ideas, theories, opinions, beliefs, practices, habits, dances and moods, which propagate within a culture. A meme propagates itself as a unit of cultural evolution, analogous in many ways to the gene (the unit of genetic information). Often memes propagate as more-or-less integrated cooperative sets or groups, referred to as memeplexes or meme-complexes. The theory itself has proved to be a successful meme, achieving penetration into popular culture, rare for a scientific theory.

Some meme-theorists contend that memes most beneficial to their hosts will not necessarily survive; rather, those memes which replicate the most effectively spread best, which allows for the possibility that successful memes might prove detrimental to their hosts. An example of this is the meme of a belief that states, "Something wonderful is about to happen." This belief may, in all rational analysis, benefit regardless of its veracity, but stronger beliefs may win out, such as the belief that "Everyone is out to get me."

If this is true, then when designing a meme (or a system of beliefs) for the purpose of Mind Control, one must consider how to increase the ability of the meme to replicate and thus increase the life span of the belief system or memeplex.

Some proponents of memes suggest that they evolve via natural selection - in a way very similar to Charles Darwin's ideas concerning biological evolution - on the premise that variation, mutation, competition and "inheritance" influence their replicative success. For example, while one idea may become extinct, other ideas will survive, spread and mutate - for better or for worse - through modification.

This has some practical applications, as you apply your skills at Mind Control. If the beliefs that you instill in people are to be of benefit to you, you need to find a way that they can persist and replicate.

One of the ways to do that is to give meaning, not just to the belief, but to holding the belief. As an example, a religious group may call themselves "believers," to emphasize the value of their belief, especially very specific beliefs in the rightness of the leader's words. Thus, as they value calling themselves "believers," then without stating it, they value the leader's words as truth.

A perhaps simpler process to accomplish replication of a meme is the initiation process. During a typical initiation, the initiate is put under emotional stress. When told he has passed the initiation, a great emotional celebration takes place. This process instills in the new initiate a deep sense of personal value for the group and the initiation. This makes him eager and willing to participate in the next initiate's ritual of initiation.

Examples of Memes:

Mormonism

Mormonism is a religion that was started in New York in the 1800s. Now it is probably best known for having originally endorsed polygamy and, while the official Mormon Church does not continue the practice, there are plenty of fundamentalist Mormons out there, who are part of a 'plural marriage.'

The original Mormons relocated from the east coast to the then secluded area that was the Utah Territory. Two factors assisted in creating a very powerful set of self-replicating memes within the Mormon culture. The first was the geographic isolation, which liberated them from the scrutiny of the rest of American culture. The second was the social isolation provided by the practice of polygamy. These factors enabled them to practice their unique form of Christianity for an entire generation, permitting those raised during this generation to see their religion as the single pathway to God.

The entire Mormon culture used its deep sense of isolation to strengthen the belief of its followers. This is reinforced by the way in which the church integrates itself into the lives of its members. From social events to youth groups, even church sanctioned life insurance companies, every aspect of life as a Mormon can be found the tentacles of church involvement.

It is often reported that when visiting Salt Lake City, Utah, the 'Vatican of Mormonism,' it is nearly impossible to live for a week amidst the people, without being asked, "Are you a member of the Church?" If you are, you get to discuss church activities; if you are not, you get to hear about how rewarding those activities are.

This is often true, even when applying for a job in Salt Lake City. While it is against the law to make an applicant's religion a basis of hiring, and even illegal to ask, many Mormon bosses find asking the question difficult to resist. In some cases, they ask about church involvement and consciously ignore the possible legal ramifications.

The memes created by the Mormon Church are ones that are designed to reinforce participation in the Church.

Example: Harley Davidson Motorcycles

Originally, Harley-Davidson built a mid-quality motorcycle. They eventually achieved a cult-like following of HOG organizations (HOG short for 'Harley Owners Group'). These groups reinforced the Harley-Davidson meme of uniqueness and supremacy, resulting in a tight bond with other Harley owners and extreme brand name loyalty.

Mind Control 101

The Example of Scientology

Like many very successful cults, Scientology has constructed around itself a very thorough belief structure. Within that belief structure is the knowledge that Scientology is the only correct path.

This belief is instilled right from the very beginning, as it teaches new recruits communication skills. During these trainings, they are taught how to calmly face the most confrontational opponent, by learning 'confrontation skills.'

Combine this belief that they are 'the way' with the skills learned about "confronting," and people will fight for the cause. In other words, it is a very powerful meme.

Do these religious memes have a higher agenda? Maybe not. The secret of using memes effectively is to create a meme that does have a higher/different agenda, but have it hidden so that it is not questioned.

An example of this is the meme created in Nazi Germany. Under Hitler, a powerful meme was created, that focused on unifying the country by creating a superior social structure, based on their idea of race. The meme itself created the Holocaust that systematically killed 6 million people (Jews, Gypsies, etc). As the meme evolved from a vision of social unity and power to mass killing, the end result became just the opposite of its original intent. It vilified 'Nazism' and turned a once spiritual symbol, the swastika, into a synonym for hate.

Because memes tend to have a life of their own, it demands a fair amount of forethought when attempting to design one.

Only Idiots are Influenced by Mind Control?

When you consider the extremes of human behavior, the most difficult actions to understand are those of seemingly normal people, who act in ways that are contrary, even to what they would think they are capable of.

Cults are the best example. No normal person would tell you that they plan to become celibate, and kill themselves in the hope to be reborn on a spaceship operated by angelic space aliens. Nonetheless, that is exactly what 39 people did in 1997, in the now famous Heavens Gate cult.

Nor would any child of a well-to-do business man leave home, with the ambition of participating in the bloody murder of a pregnant Hollywood starlet. But that is what Charles Manson compelled several of his followers to do.

When we try to make sense of these acts, we are often left dumbfounded and quickly categorize them into one of two categories: they are either "crazy" or "monsters." It is in that act that we inadvertently prevent ourselves from learning the most valuable lessons of Mind Control.

So I ask you to consider - what if they were not crazy? What if they were not a monster? What if they were, in fact, ordinary people? What would lead them to do what they did?

It is here that we come across the biggest obstacle in understanding how Mind Control works; namely, morality. Anytime that we use our morality to evaluate an action, event or situation, we unconsciously block our ability to understand it and unintentionally limit our ability to communicate effectively.

So, if you have read this far (and I know you have), it is best to put aside all your judgment and moral analysis, so as to truly learn something.

The fact of the matter is that anyone can be affected, moved and manipulated by Mind Control. Like Archimedes, who realized that if he could stand in the right place in the universe, he could move the earth, there is no man that cannot be moved, given the right pressure in the right spot at the right time.

I tell you this not to instill paranoia but humility.

Put aside your piety and judgment, and be willing to step into the minds of others, even those people you consider crazy or monstrous, and you will learn more about yourself and Mind Control than even this book can reveal.

"Whoever gets around you must be sharp and guileful as a snake; even a god might bow to you in ways of dissimulation. You! You chameleon! Bottomless bag of tricks!"
~ Homer, The Odyssey, Athena to Odysseus

So You Want to Learn to Use Mind Control?

What are the rewards of learning Mind Control?

On a lot of levels, the study of Mind Control can benefit anyone.

Mind Control 101

On the most basic level of our needs and wants, it seems simple that the more easily we can influence the people around us, the easier we will fulfill our needs for money, love, sex and security.

But that is only the most obvious. It is also the least important. While I have managed to get all of those in my life-long study of the subject, the greatest benefit I've gotten is the most difficult to quantify. It is the peace of mind that can only come from long years of using and wielding power.

Most humans hunger and long for the power that Mind Control can give. That hunger, while compelling, is also a result of lack. Not enough money. Not enough sex. Not enough certainty. Not enough security. It is like the child who is constantly trying to prove to their parents that they are good enough, even as they pass into the third, fourth and fifth decade of life.

After holding power and influence over others for a while, one quickly learns how truly simple it is. In fact, it seems that most people are walking around with their umbilical cords in their hands, seeking someone to plug it into. Power and influence are no longer goals to achieve but become tools to use. Just like a hammer in the hands of a good carpenter, who learns how to hammer a nail with the least amount of swings, so, too, power becomes something that you use less and less, as a demonstration of your skill. It is just a tool. And like the carpenter and his hammer, you can make a good living, using it effectively.

When one starts using Mind Control, the goals are usually simple and predictable; usually more sex and money. But eventually all of that becomes old and familiar. The goal then becomes finding out what the least amount of power (and Mind Control) is needed to get what you want.

Another benefit is a calm detachment from the major sufferings of humanity. One first notices it as the smug feeling of superiority that comes from knowing something that to others is forbidden. The superiority later gives way to a sense of amusement at how people make "little things" matters of life and death. They panic over rent and relationships and seeking approval.

Eventually, people will come to you asking how you remain so calm and poised amid the turmoil that seems so obvious to them. In truth, all they want is to be in the presence of that calm, because there is really nothing that you can tell them that will give them what they want.

You also learn why people who drive a Ferrari never race. It is because they don't have to.

So, what are the benefits of learning Mind Control? You tell me.

What if You Don't Learn Mind Control?

That's a great question, and I can say that, if you never learn the art of Mind Control, life will be pretty much the same. You will run with the same types of people, doing the same types of things you've always done. You will have the same frustrations that you've always had, and the same rewards.

It is very likely that, outwardly you won't appear to be missing out on anything.

Your life will be like most people, thinking that what you see is truly real, and you won't be curious or disturbed by the subtle and sometimes devious things that go on beneath the surface.

You will see people as people and, without fail, they will live up or down to your expectations.

If you don't learn Mind Control, you will continue to be distracted and annoyed by politics or advertising, but never realize or consider why.

If you never learn Mind Control, you will be able to evaluate yourself and safely conclude that you are very much like most of the people that you know, and you will be absolutely right.

What Do I Need to be Good at Mind Control?

Let's distinguish between learning Mind Control and being good at it.

Learning Mind Control falls into two categories: reading about it and studying it. As far as I know, because this book is in your hands, you are only willing to read about Mind Control. That means that you will read this book once, and remember that you read it and be able to tell people that you know something about Mind Control.

Studying Mind Control is an order of magnitude beyond reading about it. Studying means you devote yourself to understanding the concepts of Mind Control, at least on an intellectual level. Studying will make you a good commentator on the subject.

Mind Control 101

Being good at Mind Control is yet another quantum leap.

At this level, you don't just know it and can talk about it, you do it at every opportunity. You see every social interaction as an opportunity to witness some aspect of Mind Control in action or, better yet, to test something about Mind Control that you've learned.

So if you want to be good at Mind Control, it will require time and study, reading (of course) and learning the concepts, but even more, it requires an adventurous attitude and a desire to connect deeply with people.

To be good at Mind Control, it is a good idea to study everything that you can think of on hypnosis, NLP, social influence, brainwashing, cults, unclassified government documents on interrogation and more.

You will also make efforts to see Mind Control in action. You will visit and join cults. You might even try to climb the hierarchy within the cult, to see how far you can go and how much more you can learn from the experience.

You will make every attempt to make your life rich with diverse types of people, so that you can learn from experience the rules and exceptions that apply to human behavior and thought.

To truly be good at Mind Control, you must vow to live your life trying to understand and control people in ways that make them enjoy your presence and be grateful for your attention. When you screw up (and, believe me, you will), you objectively examine the results and make adjustments.

There is a mind set that anyone wanting to learn Mind Control will likely evolve to.

Curiosity

There is no limit to the amount of information about Mind Control that can be studied and tested. That is why curiosity is so important. Curiosity is the quality that will allow you to test everything that you learn about Mind Control.

Gregariousness

If you are going to learn Mind Control, you had better like being around people. This doesn't mean that you won't have a private life. In fact, a full life of personal self-discovery will certainly benefit you. The opportunity to be in the presence of other people is always taken as a chance to test your ability to guide and influence. Your goals do not have to be grand during these interactions. Sometimes it is just a matter of observing which people respond to your influence.

Studiousness

There is no limit to the aspects of Mind Control that you can study. It is assured that, as you go deeper into the depths of research and experimentation, you will uncover new and unpublished information.

Thinking Strategically - Not Just Tactically

Tactics is about the things that you do to get an outcome. Strategy is about controlling the things that influence getting your outcome. A good strategy will make it appear that the world offers you all that you want, as if it were a gift; but in fact, you have seen the real picture of what effects things. A gentle nudge, using strategy, will yield as much as a forceful push, using tactics, and make your power to appear almost magical.

Silence

This may seem counter to the mindset of gregariousness, but one finds that creating a balance between these two extremes offers great strength.

This is perhaps the most difficult part to learn: to keep silent with what you know. Many who have just learned their first magic trick are often prone to reveal the secret, in exchange for some short-term attention. In the long run, though, they lose out because, from that point on, the sense of awe you can create is replaced by the knowledge that you are a trickster. Thus one learns that keeping a secret has power, and giving it away limits that power.

"A novice chess player soon learns that it is a good idea to control the center of the board. This recognition will recur, in novel disguises, in situations far from the chessboard. It may help to seek the equivalent of the center of the board in any situation, or to see that the role of the center has migrated to the flanks, or to realize that there is no board and no singular topology."

Carl von Clausewitz, war strategist

What are the Related Fields of Mind Control?

All of the fields of Mind Control that are mentioned here have one thing in common: their goal is to change the way people think and behave.

Hypnosis

The most basic pretense of effective hypnosis is to make changes, through the bypassing of the subject's ability to analyze suggestion. When this is done, suggestions are accepted without question. What you will learn from studying hypnosis is how to make suggestions that will give your subjects the result you intended. Keep in mind that hypnosis is as much art as science, and the more you use it and test its limits, the more you will learn.

NLP

Neuro Linguistic Programming evolved from hypnosis into a very conversational form of changework and self-improvement. It creates a form of hypnotic trance, without doing the traditional hypnotic induction. Because NLP is conversational by its nature, you will learn, by studying, how to induce that hypnotic trance in a very covert fashion.

Social Influence

This is the study of how people are influenced by their interactions together. When certain aspects of their environment and interaction are altered, people will respond in certain ways. Having a good understanding of social influence will help you design the settings and environments in which people will be under your Mind Control.

Coercive Brainwashing

While this is an unpleasant subject, it should be looked into. The worst part of Coercive Brainwashing is that it lacks grace, but you will learn some creative ways that Mind Control has been used, when the subjects are incarcerated or in situations of duress.

Experimental Pharmacology

Required Disclaimer:

Neither the author nor publisher encourages the use of drugs. Drugs possess inherent dangers to the user and severe legal consequences for anyone caught giving drugs to another.

Like coercive brainwashing, using pharmacology (drugs) to influence people's thoughts and behaviors is like using a sledge hammer to crack a nut. It is overkill, for sure, but it has been used with measurable results.

Public Relations and Advertising

How do you turn sugared water into a multi-million dollar product? Call it *Coca-Cola*.

The public relations and advertising industries know exactly how to turn the thoughts of people into sales, donations and votes. Consider their incentive - money. That's enough for anyone with sufficient resources to think in terms of Mind Control.

Take some time to watch TV commercials. The more expensive the commercial, the more research the advertisers have put into their commercials. Focus groups are often used to make certain that every frame and pixel will yield the best response. Even a one-hundredth of one percent improvement can mean the difference between a million dollars' worth of profits.

Black Ops Mind Control - Stuff No One Talks About

When you consider all the speculations of conspiracy theories that are tossed about, the things they seem to have in common are minimal evidence they're real and lots of possible support information that could back them up.

What we do know for sure is that, during the Cold War, the U. S. government made a serious effort to use and understand how to control the minds of others. Most of it headed under the names MK-ULTRA and MONARCH, some information has been made available through The Freedom of Information Act.

What was revealed was that they took their job seriously. A great deal of what people say was done (and still is done) continues to fall into the arena of "plausible deniability."

There remains a lot that is strictly speculation, but there is enough material available that can allow someone to "back engineer" the various Mind Control projects that fell under these government black operations.

Psychic Influence

One can find a great deal of information on psychic influence. Unfortunately, the field of psychic influence is largely based on subjective testimonials, stories and shelves of books that wish to tell the reader how it should be done, along with the evils of doing it some other way.

Psychic influence is so subjective that what might work well for one person will cause another person headaches. If you were researching this field, the best advise is to ignore the preaching fluffy-bunny types, and test out everything to find out exactly what really works.

PART II:
The Techniques of Mind Control

Before we go into the techniques, it is probably best to think about strategy. The techniques are merely the tools and tactics to get your outcome; strategy is how you are going to use them together in a dynamic process. As a rule, most people feel they are thinking strategically, when in fact they are only thinking of tactics.

The tactics you will learn is the easy part. To get you thinking on the level of strategy, here is one Mind Control strategy to consider. It is called the Three Level Intent Strategy.

Three Level Intent Strategy

Just like it sounds, the Three Level Intent Strategy has three levels of intent: the Stated Intention, the Hidden Intention and the Secret Intention.

* The Stated Intention is what you tell people from the outset.

* The Hidden Intention is then later revealed as the deeper reason for your action. At the same time, it clouds any connection with The Secret Intention.

* The Secret Intention is the real reason for your action. It is never revealed.

Case Study

A good example of this was in the 1930s, when crime mob king pin Al Capone was approached by Count Victor Lustig and asked to invest $50,000 and was promised that the investment would double in 60 days. Capone would not usually have fallen for this, and at first thought the Count was a con-man, but there was something about him that intrigued Capone. Capone agreed to loan Lustig $50,000 and see him in two months.

At the end of the 60 days, Lustig returned to meet with Capone, and he was very disheartened. "I'm afraid things did not work out like I had thought. In fact, it was a complete failure." Capone began to consider how he would dispose of this ripoff artist.

Lustig continued by reaching in his jacket and taking out the original $50,000 and saying, "I'm terribly sorry. Here is the $50,000 you gave me. God knows I could have used the money" and got up to leave.

Capone was confused at first and then realized what he was witnessing. In all of his life of crime, he was seeing something rare - the actions of an honest man. As soon as Capone recovered his poise, he said, "I thought you were a crook at first. But you are honest! If you are in a tight spot, I hope this will help you out." Capone then peeled off $5,000 from the stack that Lustig had returned to him and handed it to him as a gift.

In fact, Count Lustig was a con-man. From the start, all he really wanted was the $5,000.

When examining this, you can see the Three Levels of Intent. The Stated Intent for Lustig was to double Capone's $50,000 in two months.

When Lustig told Capone, ""God knows I could have used the money," he was revealing the Hidden Intent - his own financial troubles.

The Secret Intent was to prove to Capone he was an honest man, and get the $5,000. As you can see, it worked wonders.

Using the Three Level Intent Strategy, you can begin to employ the techniques of Mind Control. Thinking in this way is very unnatural for most people, so the following exercise was devised.

Three Level Intent Exercise

Step 1:
Begin with your Secret Intent. Ultimately, what do you want people to do, believe or perceive?

Step 2:
Design your Stated Intent. This should be very reasonable and transparent from the outset and stated as an action that is to be performed.

Step 3:
Design a Hidden Intent that you will later reveal, or, even better, allow to be discovered. The qualities of the Hidden Intent must (1) Make the Stated Intent and your actions seem more justified and (2) Completely cloud and distance you from the Secret Intent.

It is important that you make your actions congruent with both your Stated Intent and your Hidden Intent.

Exercise Example

Your goal, or Secret Intent, is to take over your boss's business. As a Stated Intent, you say that you are going to help him improve his bottom line.

Your Hidden Intent, which is to be revealed as your work progresses, is your love of the business. You often say, "I would do this work for free. I love working with the customers so much."

As a note, often people caught stealing from the companies who hire them will attempt a version of the Three Level Intent Strategy, by appearing honest and finding needed corrections that put them into positions where they have even more access to the money. The problem is that they don't think far enough ahead. If they were truly good at stealing, they would have designed the theft, so that nothing would point to them and someone else could always be blamed.

This chapter will cover many specific methods of Mind Control. Keep in mind that there are very few instances of Mind Control that use only one technique. More often, there are numerous techniques applied in a myriad of levels.

Behavioral Conditioning
(Behavioral Modification)

In its simplest form, Behavioral Modification is nothing more than a series of rewards and punishments for certain behaviors. The goal of of Behavioral Modification is to program people to do some behaviors within certain contexts and not do other behaviors within certain contexts.

While this seems very simple, there are wonderful nuances in this field that make the application of it fascinating. To change a person's behavior is Behavioral Modification. But to train them to respond consistently is Behavioral Conditioning.

The first step is to pick the behavior you want to reinforce. Start with a small and very specific behavior. If your goal is to instill large global beliefs, then think in terms of what specific behaviors typically manifest with that belief. For example, do you want people to hold an image of a deity or guru in reverence? Then you condition them, through a series of rewards, to bow, keep silent, lower their heads or take off their shoes, while in the presence of the image.

Do you want women (or men) to give you attention? Then acknowledge them in some way that they value, when they do so.

As you compile the list of behaviors that manifest around a belief and reward them, you will be reinforcing the belief, because people will have to justify in their mind why they are behaving in such a way. While this may be obvious, the rewards should be given only in the presence of the behavior. No behavior, no reward.

Punishment can be given in the absence of the behavior, but this is best done with great care. Too many punishments that are too painful may begin to be perceived as coercion, and the subject may be responding only to avoid the punishment. In the case of reinforcing a potential lover's attention, the best punishment is an unemotional silence or simply not acknowledging that anything was said at all.

For example, if you notice that someone is typing on their computer, while you are try to talk with them, you could calmly say, "I hear you are typing. Why don't we talk, when I can get all of your attention?" If they agree to stop typing, then you can further reinforce this by saying, "No, you are preoccupied. We'll talk again," and only agree to continue the phone call, when they insist that you have their full attention.

During this exchange, there is no anger, blaming or shaming; that would be too extreme of a punishment and border on coercion. Remember, you are reinforcing the behavior first and foremost, not the emotions. The emotions will follow the behavior.

Conditioning through Behavioral Modification is the process of making the modified change a self-rewarding, self-justifying habit. This occurs with people who have been doing the same thing the same way, without variation, simply because that is how they were originally conditioned to do it.

Frequency and degree of the rewards and punishments are some of the variables to be considered, when using behavioral modification and conditioning.

Behavioral Conditioning is a fine balance of reward and punishment. While you may get quicker compliance using punishment, you will tend to get more lasting compliance with the judicious use of rewards.

The main goal of all studies of Behavioral Conditioning aim to determine the most effective ways to create a behavior and to reduce resistance to new behaviors.

Another factor to consider is the regularity of the rewards and punishments. Contrary to what might seem right, a random reward schedule gets a better response than a reward schedule that consistently gives a reward for every right action. The reason for this is that, if the subject is on a random reward schedule, they tend to learn the behavior faster. The anticipation of finding out if they get a reward adds faster learning.

Rewarding small behaviors is easier than rewarding complete change. The typical way of doing this is to ask for the behavior of your subject. Even if there is a very small change that is in the direction of your goal, it is easier to reward that and then ask for more in the future. If you deny any reward, or worse give a punishment, your subject may lose motivation.

In cults, the most common behavioral conditioning process is referred to as Love Bombing. Love Bombing takes the form of the group showing loving support and acceptance, when the subject is doing the right behavior. When the subject strays from 'right behavior,' the Love Bombing is denied and the subject is given a cold and unloving glare. The effect on the subject's behavior is visible and dramatic.

There are plenty of good books on Behavioral Conditioning, but there is no learning like that you can get from experience. Of course, you must have your objective clearly in mind, reward small behaviors that are toward your goal, and you will see it is not just easy but fun. Also, you can take an animal training course to assist you.

It is worth mentioning that there is a drawback to Behavioral Conditioning. The drawback is that its focus is on the behavior, not the motivation that drives the behavior. As a consequence, when Behavioral Conditioning is used in a therapeutic setting, the subject learns that sharing feelings about their problem is either punished or ignored. When they are rewarded, it is for things that are meaningless to them. In the end, the subject learns that withholding their feelings and their concerns is the best way to get what they want. They learn to be 'inauthentic.'

This may get the controller a desired behavioral outcome, but it would not be a lasting change.

In its highest form, Mind Control seeks to control the beliefs and motivations that drive the behaviors.

One of the very best demonstrations of this was done in 2005, by British magician, mentalist, hypnotist and performer Derren Brown, in a documentary called, "The Heist."

Under the pretense of teaching a few selected people during an exclusive "mind power seminar," he chose four people and conditioned them to hold up an armored car. Unbeknownst to them, these four were selected as being the most suggestible people from the group and, over the course of several weeks, they were conditioned so that when given an opportunity to hold up the armored car, three out of the four did it.

The armored car was merely a setup, and no laws were actually broken.

Coercion

Anything that one wishes to avoid can be used as a weapon of coercion.

Let's make it clear first that coercion is the least graceful form of Mind Control. As a technology of Mind Control, coercion is only slightly more advanced than fire. In fact, one may argue whether it is Mind Control at all, because coercion is devoid of concern about what is going on in the mind. Coercion seeks actions that are not congruent with the thoughts and feelings of the subject.

For the purposes of this book, coercion is not just a 'bad thing' but the worst thing, in terms of Mind Control, because there is no promise of long-term change. A person may be coerced into donating their money to a charity, but they are very likely to want it back in a very short amount of time.

Physical torture is the most obvious example of coercion. Torture dates back to before the Spanish Inquisition, in which people were "persuaded" into confessions of heresy. The "persuasion" was certainly painful and often lethal. Anyone who finds themselves resorting to this form of Mind Control should best read the chapter entitled, "What are the Personal Dangers of Learning Mind Control?"

Mind Control 101

Mental/Emotional Torture

Providing mental and emotional discomfort to influence people's actions is another form that falls under the heading 'Torture,' though it is often more indirect and less obvious. In this category, there is no physical discomfort, but mental and emotional stress is applied.

A good example of this is a police interrogation, where they knowingly employ the most thorough tools of Mind Control to get the information they need.

This begins innocently enough. They ask their suspect to enter into a room "just to clear up a few questions." From that point on, the suspect is under isolation and completely under their influence. They will alternate between letting him know that he's not in trouble and that they think he is withholding information and could be arrested for doing so. The interrogators will ask seemingly unrelated questions, as if they were of vital importance. The mental stress and confusion, combined with long hours of question asking (see 'Gaslighting') loosens the suspect's hold on his perceptions, just enough to reveal information that will be presented at his own trial.

In some cases, innocent people have succumbed to the pressure and confessed to things they did not do.

From this example, the question should be asked, "Do police lie to get the information they need?" You bet they do. Police will go to any pretense, to get the information they need.

A more severe form of this type of Mind Control is military interrogation.

In the event of their capture, every Special Forces soldier and military pilot is required to be part of the receiving end of a military interrogation, as part of their training. This takes the form of 'Escape and Evade' training, which incorporates the most severe forms of coercion and duress. Prior to this training, they are warned that, during the mock military interrogation, they will go through to "Believe half of what you see and none of what you hear." Even given this warning, the control that 'the enemy" interrogators have is so deep and pervasive, that most of the trainees accept the lies told to them as truths.

Outside of the isolated environment of an interrogation room, emotional coercion is quite common. It takes the form of passive-

Mind Control 101

aggressive behavior, outbursts of anger, blaming, threats to withhold love and attention or visitation privileges, etc.

As a general rule, coercive practices of Mind Control have the opposite long-term effect. Where the operator wants trust, it creates suspicion; where love is desired, it creates fear and so on. If you remember back to the Three Level Intent Strategy, the only real use of coercion in long-term Mind Control is if you want your Secret Intent to be fear, suspicion, etc, while justifying your coercive with your Hidden Intent. This is typical passive aggressive behavior.

Game Theory

An interesting concept came out of game theory that can be used to create incredible motivation in people. This is a type of coercion, even though the people had to volunteer for the situation, and they knew the structure of the situation from the outset.

The people all wanted to lose 10 to 15 lbs of weight in 6 weeks time. They all had trouble keeping to their diets.

The experiment was very simple. They were told that, if they did not lose the weight, semi-nude photos of themselves would be published and sent to people that they know. They were not told how to diet, only that if they didn't lose the weight, there would be definite embarrassing consequences.

Remember these were volunteers.

The percentage of people who reached their goal weight within the deadline was over 90%.

Thinking about it, the reason is very simple. They had a visible and quantifiable consequence, if they did not lose the weight.

The ancient Chinese war strategist Sun Tzu referred to this as 'the death ground,' where an army is stuck between a cliff face and an opposing force that seeks to destroy them. Their only option is to fight with all their hearts.

As for using this as a Mind Control tool, it gives renewed meaning to the word 'deadline' and is often used by employers, to hasten the completion of a project.

Whether the threat is real or fabricated, they will say that the project must be completed by a deadline, or the company will close (or some other tangible threat). As a positive effect, when this tactic is successfully used within a group, it can bring an esprit de corps that helps unify the members as 'brothers in arms.'

To use this technique effectively, it is fairly simple: 1) The consequence of failure must seem real, measurable and immediate; 2) It must affect the subjects on a personal level; 3) It must be believable.

Social Pressure & Mob Mind Control

I was watching a TV show on how groups of strangers come together, to become a riotous mob. What I saw was clearly an altered state of group consciousness.

"None of us is dumber than all of us." - Anonymous

Being the deviant thinker that I am, I immediately asked, "How could this mob mentality be used and exploited?"

The first step is to do an analysis of the dynamic.

The members of the mob share one thing in common.

Of these, you can see that some of it comes about from having a common enemy:

* Anger over a vetoed bill
* Soccer fan angry at an opposing team
* AIDS or PETA activists

But others have more benevolent common factors:

* A vacation beach
* A victory rally for their local sports team
* The start of a peaceful demonstration

For the individual participants, who become "the mob" and operate outside of their normal behaviors, there are some common qualities that can be isolated:

* They have an opportunity to freely express their most base emotions, while being protected by the anonymity of "the crowd."

* A very small group (sometimes only one person) of these most active participants tend to elicit participation from others.

* Alcohol is often a factor, further loosening inhibitions that turn someone over to mob control. (See the section on Pharmacology & Mind Control).

Another factor to consider is that counter measures to control the mob (riot police banging night sticks against plexiglass shields, for example) often bring about an escalation in mob violence. This is especially true when the police represent the oppressive government or force, which the group is protesting against.

This is just a hypothetical conjecture, of course, but how could one use these factors to create a mob that would do what you wanted? First, the outcome should be clearly stated. Because mob mentality is almost on the level of an idiot, one must set the bar pretty low, and make clear simple tasks that one would only do behind the cover of anonymity. These don't have to be malicious acts, but malicious act are easier to create.

The Steps for Mob Mind Control

1. Have a clear and simple outcome for your mob to perform. Don't tell them ahead of time.
2. Create a shared experience in a location where the action should take place.
3. Create a heightened emotional state in the group. Anger is an easy state to elicit, but more positive states can work as well.
4. Isolate potential mob leaders, who would more freely act if protected by anonymity of the crowd.
5. Call to action. Make it simple.
6. Keep the group together.
7. As the mob actions escalates, others can be brought in by rumor exchange. Given the group dynamic by introducing an emotional rumor, true or not, other more docile members of the group can be called in to contact with the front lines. Screaming, "They just killed a kid with their night sticks!" is a good example.
8. If you only want chaotic destruction, it will be easy, and all you have to do is add lots of alcohol to the above equation.

Because violent mob action is well documented more benevolent mob reactions would be interesting to study.

One example of a very benevolent mob act is a fad called 'an event' that uses cell phones and web sites to solicit strangers to take part in innocuous "public performance art." One example of such an event is everyone who subscribes to the service is asked to go to the third floor of Macy's in New York City at a specific time and ask all the clerks, "Where do you keep the underwear drawer?" Then at a prescribed time the group disperses as fast as they came.

Another example is Burning Man, an annual week-long bacchanal set in the desert, that culminates in the burning of a large effigy. In that event, the emotion and drug use is often very high. Burning Man could be excluded from this type of mob chaos, because of its well-structured, ritualistic nature.

These 'events' fill most of the requirements for a mob act, except the extreme emotional state. It could be assumed then that, for some mob actions, anonymity and an emotional state of mischievousness are sufficient to bring some action about.

A further assumption is that the more intense the emotion, especially true of emotions of fear and anger, the more volatile the potential behavior of the mob.

What could be an application of this knowledge?

Violent Organized Group Ritual

This seems most obvious to me. Creating a highly organized event in which violence, destruction and 'chaos' is systematically structured into the situation and allowed, under proper circumstances. Control of the violence could be made by several modifications. The first being removal of any outside elements to interfere with the ritual. Plus rules for the engagement, like in the film Fight Club and at Burning Man, that would swiftly deal with only the individuals and not the crowd.

Marketing

Scheduling various "events," like the one mentioned at Macy's, could be used to bring some emphasis to the consumer's need for a product and raise stock prices.

Political Action

Already been done.

AIDS activists blocked off the Golden Gate Bridge to gain attention for their cause.

Counter-Marketing

Hold an event, and sell cheaply or give away beer, in the name of your competitor. Get the crowd drunk, then insult them, and stop selling beer to the angry crowd. This would create a bad rep for your competitor. Make certain there are lots of things for the crowd to destroy, that has your competitor's name on it.

Demolition

This would be an interesting experiment. Start a demonstration around an old house you want torn down. Incite a drunken fraternity party riot, and have the mob destroy the house. Liability would go largely to the fraternity.

Social Influence a la Robert Cialdini

Social Influence is the study of how people can affect each other, when interacting with each other.

The scientific study of the process of social influence has been underway since the 1940s, beginning in earnest with the propaganda, public information and persuasion programs of World War II. Since that time, numerous social scientists have studied the ways in which one individual can influence another's attitudes and actions.

The powerful effects of social influence was first published in the book, "Influence: How and Why People Agree to Things," by Dr. Robert Cialdini.

In the book, Dr. Cialdini describes six factors that lead people to do things that they wouldn't ordinarily do, under most other circumstances. This can have a very dramatic impact, when used alone and even more when combined with other tactics of Mind Control.

Reciprocity

The act of simply giving a gift, without expectation, has a very powerful effect on people. Remember the phrase, "There is no such thing as a free lunch."

All societies subscribe to a norm that obligates its members to repay in kind what they have received. So when one is approached by someone on the street, giving them a flower, they are much more likely to give a donation in return, when asked. It is a common practice among groups soliciting for donations.

Evangelist Oral Roberts is famous for his lucrative letter-writing campaigns to his followers. One such letter included a one inch square of carpet, that he described as being from his old office. "Over the last 15 years, I have knelt and prayed for hours on this carpet," the letter would say. At the conclusion, he would ask for a donation - and it worked!!

Reciprocity is used in most Mind Control settings. The important thing to understand is that the item that you are giving does not need to be of any great value. It is the act of freely giving it that makes the impact. Give the item, and mention that it is free and there is no obligation, then ask for something. Don't put any focus on the gift; they can keep it no matter what.

A gift can also be a concession of some sort. Knowing this, you can offer them something that you know might be too expensive for them, like a large donation or giving of their time. When they refuse to acknowledge their misgivings, and lower the offer, ask for less.

Exercise in Reciprocity

Anytime you know that you are going to ask for something - *anything* - create an opportunity to give the person something, before you ask. Make sure there is no obligation connected to the gift; you just thought they might like it. The gift can be relatively insignificant. If for any reason they refuse, don't take back the gift or bring it to their attention.

Commitment & Consistency

Anytime you ask a person to do something, even the most small and insignificant action, you begin the process of creating some form of consistent action that they can continue. This is most easily done by requesting that someone do something small, then later asking them for just a little bit more. In doing this, they will try to act consistently with their previous actions. The magnitude of the requests can escalate, until more and more is given.

Consider the so-called 'brainwashing' of American soldiers by the Chinese military, during the Korean War. During an interrogation, they would ask simple, easy to answer questions, like, "What is your name and rank?" The soldier could easily answer these questions. Often, they were then asked to talk about their life back home in the United States. Again, an easy request, which might be rewarded with some small privilege or some extra food. They were then asked to talk about the things they didn't like about back home - taxes, unfair treatment by their local police, legal problems, etc.

Each time they would give forth more and more information, until they were directed by the questioning to not like the unfair treatment they are now recognizing by the U. S. government. Through the use of consistency, they would eventually be willing to completely denounce the U. S. government and its military policies.

The key here is to ask something small of the person or persons you are trying to affect, then slowly escalate the requests.

An example of this in action was used by a restaurant, to ensure patrons would call, if canceling a reservation. The change dropped his no-call, no-show rate from 30 to 10 percent, immediately.

All that was done was to change a simple question. The receptionist only had to change her request from, "Please call, if you have to change your plans" to "Will you please call, if you have to change your plans?" At that point, she politely paused and waited for a response. The wait was pivotal, because it induced customers to fill the pause with a public commitment. And public commitments, even seemingly minor ones, direct future action.

Exercise in Commitment & Consistency

Keep your outcome in mind. Find something you can ask of someone that is small and insignificant. Later, ask them for something slightly more. Test this out on others, without asking for the first, smaller request. Note their responses.

Social Proof

In short, Social Proof is doing something, because everyone else is doing it. Don't underestimate its effectiveness.

If one person stands looking up into the air, there is a only a small chance that anyone else will look up, trying to discover what that person is looking at. If there are three or four people looking up in the same direction, the numbers of people who comply and gaze upward has been shown to quadruple.

This effect of Social Proof can be easily incorporated, by having the Mind Control subject in the presence of people, who are already conforming to the prescribed 'acceptable behavior.' This has particular power with people who feel they are outside the social norm, and find a group that is accepting and non-judgmental toward them. If the group is designed to appeal to those 'outside the norm,' those joining in the activities will be even more likely to conform to the new behaviors.

The more you can show evidence that "everyone is doing it," the more effective a demonstration of social proof you have.

Consider how a party can start, and turn into an orgy. If there are enough people willing to take part, the more inhibited individuals will feel more comfortable to take part.

Liking

Liking demonstrates the tendency for people to participate in activities, in which their friends are also participating. A Tupperware party is a great example of that.

Likewise, liking can come about by more superficial means. Attractive people can more easily flirt their way to success in more ventures than the unattractive. This is not lost to members of cults, who tell their most attractive members to guide the curious into the next level of indoctrination.

There are many self-improvement workshops that rely on this, by insisting their participants enlist their friends to take the next training.

Authority

Getting someone who is perceived as an authority will add value to a product or service. Having Charlton Heston as the president of the Nation Rifle Association was a great victory, because if Moses/Ben Hur/Charlton Heston is a member, it must be good.

This is the power of testimonials. As a tool of Mind Control, there is a hierarchy of value of these testimonials. In order of value, they are:

1. Pictures of several celebrities with testimonials
2. Picture of a single celebrity with testimonial
3. Pictures of several ordinary people with their testimonials
4. Testimonials of ordinary people with their full names and locations
5. Testimonials lacking information of names and locations

Exercise in Using Authority

Consider what your message is or what you want your subjects to do. What perceived authority can you point to, who endorses your outcome?

Scarcity

A great deal of evidence shows that items and opportunities become more desirable to us, as they become less available. For this reason, marketers trumpet the unique benefits or the one-of-a-kind character of their offerings. It is also for this reason that they consistently engage in 'limited time only' promotions, or put us into competition with one another, using sales campaigns based on 'limited supply.'

Scarcity can take several forms: limited supply, limited time to join/buy/participate, limited membership and limited to only the people who qualify.

Exercise in Scarcity

First, examine every instant when scarcity is used on you. You will find it everywhere, with "limited time offer" and "call within the next 15 minutes and..." and more.

Consider your message or product and how you can add scarcity to increase its value. If the product is you and your image, the rule often is, "The guru at the bottom of the hill doesn't have a following." Find ways to make yourself inaccessible.

NLP - Neuro Linguistic Programming

NLP is short for Neuro-Linguistic Programming and is the most contemporary, publicly available system of Mind Control.

NLP came about from therapists that were able to accomplish their therapeutic goals in very short periods of time. Not only has NLP proved to be an effective therapeutic tool, it is also a very powerful covert tool of persuasion and influence. If a therapist can subtly persuade a client to accept a new solution to their problem, then the same techniques can be used to sell a product or even instill a new list of beliefs.

As much as NLP is a science, it is also an art, and it takes a good understanding of the NLP model and techniques, as well as the time to practice it.

To understand the model of NLP, one first has to accept that, in many ways, people are both the same and different. We are the same, in that we have only a limited number of ways to understand our experience. We are different, in that each person has their own specific way of making sense of their experience. For the individual who knows how someone else makes sense of their world, they can tailor their message, so that it is accepted.

Needless to say, with the power that is implied in NLP, it has been picked up and exploited in the fields of sales, advertising and in helping men get laid.

Sensory Acuity

Sensory acuity is NLP lingo for "Pay Attention!"

It basically means, when working with someone, that you have to pay more attention to how they are responding than whether or not you are doing things right. When you do that ("Pay Attention!"), you will notice that people respond to you in very subtle ways.

Rapport

For the purpose of Mind Control and NLP, the best place to start is at the beginning. All NLP teaching starts with the topic of rapport.

Rapport is much more than just having someone like you. In fact, it is possible to have rapport with someone who doesn't like you. What is important about rapport is that the other person perceives that you are very much like them, on a deep level. This allows the person to feel comfortable with you and willing to respond to you, with some sense of acceptance. (Yes, even if they don't like you, they can be responsive to you. Think of this as enemies who respect each other.)

It's been said, and rightly so, that without rapport nothing is possible, and with rapport anything is possible.

Mirroring & Matching

"Mirroring and Matching" are the techniques that are first learned to create rapport.

Mirroring simply means to move and speak in a manner that is like the other person and doing it in a way that doesn't appear like mimicry. This creates an unconscious belief in the other person that you are like them.

You can see people unconsciously mirroring each other, among those who already are in rapport. They sit the same way; when one changes his position, the other person will change their position to match the other person. It is a very natural outcome of having rapport.

Many NLP trainings spend long hours doing mirroring and matching exercises, to help participants learn to gain rapport quickly. The exercises are very useful, but there is an easier way.

The easier way to gain rapport is to think of mirroring as a result of rapport, instead of the cause of it. In other words, when you like someone and feel you are like this person, you have rapport and will do all the mirroring and matching, without thinking about it. So, all you have to do is assume you are like this person. Assume that the rapport is already there and that you both have a deep familiarity with the other person's thoughts and habits. At first, this may take some mental gymnastics, but it is much easier than paying close attention to people's movements and then moving your body to match theirs.

Rapport Exercise 1:

Find a person you don't know well, and begin a conversation with them, while mirroring the body position and movements. In order not to get caught, make sure you wait five seconds after they have moved, before you move into their body posture and position.

Rapport Exercise 2:

Do the exercise above, but this time, assume you already have rapport with the other person. This means starting off in your mind with the assumption that you like this person and have known them for a long time and that you will naturally get along.

* * * * * * * *

By doing these exercises, you will learn the power of rapport and hopefully gain some respect for how difficult Mind Control is. There is also a likelihood that you will begin to see people as unique individuals and not just objects to be manipulated. In spite of the fact you want to control their minds, this last point is actually a benefit to you, because it will help put a velvet glove over the iron fist of power you are trying to wield.

Pacing & Leading

Pacing and leading can be used in any situation, in many different ways.

Pacing and leading consists of first *pacing*, which essentially means the controller does what the other person is doing; then followed by *leading*, doing something that takes the lead, so that the subject can follow.

Using pacing and leading is an essential part of traditional rapport exercises, as mentioned above. In the case of rapport, the controller would pace the movements of the subject, then later lead.

Pacing and leading can also be used in just about any situation, in order to take the lead.

Linguistically, pacing and leading take the form of 1) a pace, anything that is true and verifiable by the subject and 2) a lead, which is a statement that the controller wishes the subject to agree upon. The traditional formula for this type of pacing and leading is:

Pace, pace, pace, lead. Pace, pace, lead.
Pace, lead.
Lead, lead lead....

It would sound something like this:

Here we are (pace).... You are sitting here (pace)... and we're talking (pace)... and there is something curious happening that you might not be aware of (lead).... Time is passing (pace).... It always does (pace).... We forget what is really important (lead).... But we're here (pace)... and when you focus in on what is important (lead)... you can give it strength and see it (lead)... as if it were right in front of you (lead).... You can feel how this moves you (lead)... because it is that important (lead)... and you know it (lead)....

Pacing & Dragging

This refers to something a little bit more intense than pacing and leading. It requires strong sensory acuity and the ability to compel the subject to follow your lead, much earlier than would normally occur with pacing and leading.

Pacing and Dragging require several things from the operator:

* Focus - Focus means that the operator is completely focused on the subject and intentionally ignores any of their own personal concerns, whatever they may be. As the controller, this means that bills, mortgage payments, fights with spouses are put completely aside, when you are with your subject.

* Concern - As a controller, Concern means making the subject the most important person in your world, while you are with them. This can only be done by using your focus and sense of caring, even if you have to fake it.

Passion & Conviction

Passion and Conviction is the knowledge that what you are doing is right. There are very few things more powerful than the belief in what you are doing.

To enliven this belief, consider all the benefits of what you are doing that involves the subject. These benefits include reasons why it is important, and it also includes the values or things that it gives you.

By combining these qualities, pacing and dragging is made easier. Sensory acuity will be heightened by the focus and concern and can be used to see if the subject is in any way resisting the leading/dragging. When resistance is sensed, the controller can make immediate corrections to their presentation.

The Power of Physiology

Physiology in NLP terms means how the body is used to create and lead emotional and mental states. By making changes in the physiology, it is much easier to access certain emotional states.

A good example of this is the act of simply sitting up straight and looking upward. It is very, very hard for anyone to maintain a depressed state, as they do this.

On the other hand, one will tend to find that, by slumping over, looking downward and breathing very short and shallow breaths, depression is easy to achieve. It is a freaking wonder more people haven't applied this. But good Mind Controllers have.

Consider how may churches have very high and ornate ceilings. This forces the people to look up and more easily access pleasant emotional states.

Another way of utilizing physiology is for the controller to simply tell the subject what to do and how to posture themselves. Rituals, meditations and breathing exercises are all designed to covertly affect the subjects' physiology, to aid in an outcome.

By simply asking, "Can I show you something about how your body effects your mind?" a controller can then ask the subject to change their posture or movements, in order to demonstrate the point.

Public speakers and seminar leaders will often make sure the audience is in their control, by asking them, as a group, to do certain simple changes to their posture - asking them to sit up straight, breathe as if they are very excited, and sit on the edge of their seats (literally), as if what they are going to hear is the most important information they'll ever hear.

The key factors of physiology that are within conscious control are posture, breathing, eye movement and activity. So by effecting any combination of these, a change in emotions can occur.

Physiology Exercise

Monitor your mood and emotional state. Determine what mood you want to be in, and adjust your posture and physiology to fit that mood. This may include sitting up straight, tilting your chin up and looking up. Experiment with putting a slight smile on your mouth.

Physiology Exercise II

Ask a friend to participate in an exercise with you. You can say, "Can I show you something about how your body affects your mind?" to start, and see how many emotional states you can lead them through. Start with contrasting emotions: depression/joy, anger/acceptance, fear/excitement, hate/joy, revulsion/attraction.

When doing this, make sure that the positive states are elicited when they are looking at you, and the negative emotions are elicited while NOT looking at you, or with eyes closed. This will link good feelings to you.

Physiology Exercise III

Create a ritual or activity that allows a reason for the subject to make changes in breathing, eye movement, posture and activity. It can include music, dance, drumming or exercise.

Sensory Modalities & Sub-Modalities

In NLP, one interprets reality through the senses, and usually one of the senses is dominant. Visual/sight, auditory/hearing and kinesthetic/feeling are the main modes (or modalities) that people use. These are preferred ways of thinking that people use, and in NLP literature, is referred to as VAK - for Visual, Auditory, Kinesthetic.

People who think predominately in *visual* terms will refer to something as how they "see" things, and use phrases like, "That seems right," "It is clear to me," "I've good a picture of what you are saying."

A person who thinks in *auditory* terms will say things like, "That sounds like a good idea," "Let me chime in," "That speaks to me."

A person who thinks in kinesthetic terms will respond to how things *feel,* and use phrases like, "I've got a gut feeling about this," "Get a grip on it," "That has impact."

All one has to do to determine someone's dominant sensory modality is listen to them speak. Therefore, sensory acuity is very important.

When you use a person's predominate sensory modality, you increase rapport and gain a greater foothold to guide them.

More Sensory Modality Information

Ask someone how they decided to make their last purchase, and listen to what they say. In making decisions, people will go through a mental process, in which they mention, in order, the sensory modalities they use.

For example, if you are showing someone a coat to buy, and ask them how they got their last coat, and they say, "I saw (visual) the coat in the window and said (auditory) to myself, 'That looks good.' Then I got this feeling (kinesthetic) that I had to have it."

To keep rapport, all you have to do is use that same process. For example, "Take a look (visual) at this coat, and when you do, listen (auditory) for "That looks good," and tell me how good a feeling (kinesthetic) you get."

Sub-modalities

Sub-modalities are more specific distinctions of the various sensory modalities. When these sub-modalities are altered, the impact of the message is also altered.

Of the visual modality, some of the sub-modalities are the distance of an image, the size, location, whether it is in color or black and white, location of the image. These are the most prominent and common enough for most to use effectively.

Auditory sub-modalities include loudness, if it is a voice that one is hearing or telling themselves (it usually is), gender of the voice, emotional tone, direction/location, whispering, speed of voice.

Kinesthetic sub-modalities include, warmth, heaviness, location in the body, tingly, soft, hard, etc.

To understand how sub-modalities are used therapeutically, consider how someone might describe being depressed. Their head lowers, and their physiology slumps (kinesthetic). They hear a loud oppressive voice in their mind saying, "You are worthless!" Then they hear their own voice say, "I'm nothing." Then they see an image of themselves standing two feet tall and stared at with contempt, by everyone who sees them (visual).

The therapist using NLP would elicit this information, which the subject is not consciously aware of, and then have the subject consciously alter these sub-modalities. The subject would start by envisioning themselves as standing very tall and having people seeing them and smiling (visual). The internal voices would be turned to giggling whispers, with louder more positive voices saying, "You are the best!" Added (auditory). Kinesthetically, they would be asked to "stand taller" and imagine positive feelings within their body.

This will have an immediate effect on the subject, but it may be only temporary, unless it is practiced as an ongoing project.

As a tool of Mind Control, one can use sub-modalities covertly, by using some general rules about sub-modalities that tend to effect most people.

Visual sub-modalities tend to have more impact on people when they are imagined close-up, large and in color. So by describing your product or service as being "big" and seeing it "up close and colorful" will tend to make most impact.

As an example, note the difference between these two apartment-for-rent listings:

Two bed room, one bath apartment. Dining space with kitchen area." or "Spacious, colorful two bedroom apartment with sunlit dining space. Second bedroom suitable for a bright home office."

Note how the second description makes the apartment seem more real. This can be used for Mind Control, by adding more visual sub-modalities to the description of your product or service.

Television commercials and print ads often make use of this, by showing their product as large and colorful as possible and comparing their competitor in smaller black and white images.

Describing auditory sub-modalities as loud and echoing will tend to have a strong impact, but you must be cautious with this, as some people will not respond positively to a "loud" description.

Mind Control 101

The kinesthetic sub-modalities of "warm" "soft" "comforting" and "embracing" tend to be thought of as positive to most people. Sub-modalities of "sharp" "cutting" "rigid" "chilling" tend to be considered negative.

To add impact to any message, a Mind Control operator can use a very effective process of incorporating the visual, auditory and kinesthetic sub-modalities to all of their communications. This will make certain that people will see, hear and feel the message impact, regardless of their dominant sensory modality.

Values Elicitation

Values are the core of our decision making. They are deep and unconscious, until they are either fulfilled or challenged.

Values are powerful enough that when someone tells you that, by buying their product or service, your values will be fulfilled, it is almost impossible to resist. To a sales person, finding someone's values is equivalent to finding their buy-button and pressing it again and again.

Using values as a Mind Control tool is powerful enough that, if you don't fulfill them as you promise, you will make a very bad enemy - so use this tool wisely.

The process of using values as a tool of Mind Control consists of uncovering a persons values and then linking them to your outcome. Both steps are amazingly simple and straightforward.

The Elicitation

First, understand that everyone has criteria that needs to be fulfilled, before they agree to something. If it is a new car, they may need it to be fast, or a new model, or color or within a certain price range. Once these criteria are are met, the person feels the value.

Most people try to influence by trying to meet all the criteria. Values elicitation bypasses that and goes straight for that motivating value.

Getting to the value is done by simply asking the question, "What's important about (fill in your product)?" For example, if you are trying to enroll someone in a communication workshop, you would ask, "What's important about communicating with people?" From that, you will get their first answer. Then you ask them, "What's important about that (their first answer)?" giving you their second answer. Then ask, "What is important about that (their second answer)?" Usually, by then, you will have reached their highest value. Don't be surprised if they show some sort of strong emotion.

Let me give you some advise on asking these questions. Keep in mind, you don't want to learn why it is important, only what is important about "it." The reason is that "why?" causes people to become defensive. To make it simple, don't ask, "Why is important?!"

While asking these questions, it is important to not make it sound like an interrogation. You can do this by interspersing your questions with conversations about life and relevant matters.

What you will notice is that, when you show a sincere curiosity about what is important to people, people take interest. To say it another way, asking these questions builds rapport, because people like to talk about what they feel is important.

Another way to accomplish an elicitation of values is to simply listen. Many people will quickly begin to talk about what they value. If you simply feed that back to them and ask them to elaborate, you will find that they "light up" - a strong indication that you have gotten to something they value.

The Delivery of Values Elicitation

Once you have their values, the rest is fairly simple. All you have to do is mention those values, as you describe your service or product.

Saying, "Do you feel that having X and Y and Z are important enough to take part in this seminar?"

Or, while this may be crude, you can say, "This seminar shows you how to have more X,Y and Z. Does it sound like something you'd like to take part in?"

Final Note on Values Elicitation

This process is so powerful that you have to really try it to test its effectiveness. You should also note that, if your product or service doesn't fulfill that value as you've implied, you may have a very upset person. In fact, enemies are made by cheating them in this fashion. Beware.

Mind Control 101

Determining Values Through Surveys

To find out people's values on a large scale, some people will employ a survey that asks various questions about certain aspects of their lives. From this information one can tailor responses and presentations prior to individual meetings.

Emotional Elicitation

Emotional Elicitation is the NLP process of bringing out the emotions you want an individual to feel. It will be of great value in the next section on anchoring.

To start, determine what emotions in your subject would help lead to your outcome. These emotions could be excitement, joy, fear, worry, frustration, despair, love, certainty, curiosity etc.

There are several ways to elicit emotions. The simplest and the most direct way is to ask, "What is it like when you feel X?" or "Do you remember a time when you felt?" Keep in mind that rapport is vital to doing this process, because these are rather strange questions to be asking a stranger. So, gain rapport!

As you ask these questions, watch how they respond. You should be able to witness the emotion emerge.

Another way to do this is by talking about the feeling, as if you are telling a story, describing the emotion. Use your sensory acuity when doing this, as it doesn't promise that your description will match your subject's, so pay attention to how they react.

By doing emotional elicitation successfully, it causes the subject to be a bit more flexible. If they are able to bring about emotions that you lead them to, it is an indication you have great rapport and makes them even more responsive to your leading. This is often done in TV shows and what makes watching certain series so addictive. Yes, the media knows the power of Mind Control.

Emotional Elicitation in Writing

Emotional elicitation happens all the time in writing and is most common in fiction, because it allows the reader to identify with a character and become emotionally involved.

You will also see emotional elicitation in the very best advertising.

Anchoring

Anchoring is the next step, once you've learned how to elicit emotions.

Anchoring is a very Pavlovian procedure that links an emotion to a gesture, a touch, an object or setting or anything at all. It is a very natural process that we, as humans, have anchors. We love our favorite restaurant, because they treated us right and left us with a warm feeling every time we think about it. Commercials use the anchoring process by eliciting an emotion and then linking the feeling to a product.

To use anchoring, your sensory acuity must be sharp enough to notice when someone is feeling the emotion you are trying to elicit. As the emotion climbs to a peak, you "set" the anchor, meaning to bring in the thing you want to associate with the feeling.

Consider how anchoring happens in a romantic setting. Rapport is built, and warm and fuzzy feelings start to grow, as you are looking at the person. This, alone, links those feelings to the person, so that all you have to do is think of the persons face, and you feel those feelings.

But you can use this to accelerate those feelings, by using the anchoring process with a conscious intention.

One way that can be accomplished is to first elicit the feeling, either through asking about what it is like to feel a "connection" with someone, or by describing the connection (or both). As you notice the feeling within the person grow, you touch them in a unique way.

Here is a word-for-word example of romantic anchoring that is often used in romantic settings:

I don't know what it is that causes most people to notice that feeling of connectedness to each other. One of my friends was telling me that, when she can feel that connection, it is like there is this cord of light that connects us (gesture by moving the hand between you and the other person, simulating the connection), and this cord grows with the warmth of that connection. I imagine that it is like you feel this "click," and you can see yourself years from now and still feel that connection... and then remember back to today as the start of it. And you can feel that right here (touch the solar plexus of the other person).

The touch to the solar plexus will anchor that feeling of

connection (referred to as "setting the anchor"). So any time you want to bring about that feeling again, all you need to do is touch the solar plexus, and the feeling will return.

Other ways of setting anchors can be done without physical contact. Using a unique gesture, like tilting your head, or stroking your chin will work just as well.

In NLP lingo that second touch that brings back the emotion is called "firing the anchor."

Anchoring Exercise 1

Watch TV commercials for the use of anchoring. You will notice it anytime some strong emotion is raised. Typically within the first 30 seconds, an emotion will be elicited from the viewer, and the commercial will end with either the name of the product or the product logo.

Anchoring Exercise 2

Create a conversation with someone, with the outcome of setting and firing an anchor. Determine the emotion that you want to elicit and a unique way of setting and firing the anchor. Practice until you become good at it. Remember to use your sensory acuity. Note: be fearless, and don't worry about being caught. Learn from your mistakes.

Embedded Commands

Embedded Commands are incredibly effective as a tool of Mind Control, because they deliver messages to the unconscious mind, without the conscious mind being aware of it.

You can think of them as almost subliminal, except that when you are trained to listen for them, they become quite obvious. Thankfully, almost no one devotes enough time to learn to use or listen for embedded commands.

To learn how to use embedded commands, consider first how we speak. We tend to say things with one specific voice or tone of voice. Occasionally, we get excited or angry, and our voice will change in volume or intensity, but for the most part, we speak without much change in our modulation and pace.

Embedded commands work by using our voice to mark off certain words and phrases in our speech, so that we are sending two messages. One of them is conscious and one is unconscious.

The conscious message is the basic content of what we are saying. This would be the information that would be conveyed, if we were to write down our words and read them from a script.

The unconscious messages are the short words and phrases that you mark off as commands, by changing the delivery of your words.

For example, let's use the quote from above. This time, the words that are to be used as embedded commands are marked in **bold**.

*I don't know what it is that causes most people to **notice that feeling of connectedness** to each other. One of my friends was telling me that when she can **feel that connection** it is like there is this cord of light that connects us and this cord grows with the warmth of that connection. I imagine that it is like you **feel this "click"** and you can **see yourself years from now** and **still feel that connection**... and then **remember back to today** as the start of it. And you can **feel that right here**.*

As you make a list of the phrases in bold, you will see a theme.

"notice that feeling of connectedness"
"feel that connection"
"feel this 'click'"
"see yourself years from now"
"feel that connection"
"remember back to today"
"feel that right here"

Because these are parts of complete sentences, you can significantly change how the phrases are pronounced to mark them off, but there will be no conscious awareness of anything being any different.

There are several ways to pronounce the phrases differently from the rest of the paragraph, so that the unconscious mind begins to recognize the patter. The easiest way is to pause before the embedded command; then lower your voice; then pause after the end of the command, and resume to normal speaking.

Try reading it again this time, and note that the "..." marks indicate a pause, and when you read the command, read it like you are giving a command, and let the tonality drop, as if giving an order.

I don't know what it is that causes most people to ...notice that feeling of connectedness... to each other. One of my friends was telling me that when she can ...feel that connection... it is like there is this cord of light that connects us... (gesture by moving the hand between you and the other person, simulating the connection) and this cord grows with the warmth of that connection. I imagine that it is like you ...feel this "click"... and you can ...see yourself years from now... and still ...feel that connection... and then ...remember back to today... as the start of it. And you can ...feel that right here... (touch the solar plexus of the other person).

At first, using embedded commands will seem awkward and unnatural. Get over it. This is a tool that people have paid a lot of money to learn for good reason - it works. If you follow the steps of the exercises below, you will become very good at embedded commands, and you will see people responding to your commands, without even knowing what's going on.

1. State your outcome not just in terms of actions but also in terms of emotions that motivate the action.
2. Write short 2 to 4 word commands that lead to your outcome. The more the better.
3. Write as many of these commands as possible.
4. Make sure they are in command form.
5. Begin to write the commands into a monologue about anything you would normally be talking about.
6. Read it aloud.
7. Practice, practice, practice.

Using only one embedded command will not be effective, because the subject's unconscious mind will not have enough samples of the commands to distinguish it as different from the rest of the speech, and determine that these are commands. So the rule is to use a lot of them.

Because embedded commands are covert, it is possible to send them to one person in a group, by marking the commands with a direct eye-contact gaze to the subject.

Meta Programs

A Meta Program is an NLP term that describes the possible ways individuals sort the information they perceive. Thus they can determine an appropriate reaction.

It has been stated by some that there are over 30 various Meta Programs that people unconsciously use. In this chapter, I'll restrict this to the six most common and most easily understandable Meta Programs.

The NLP model Meta Programs demonstrate that we can best interact with (and control) people, if we deal with them as they are, instead of forcing them to be what we think they ought to be.

Keep in mind that all Meta Programs are dependent on the context and not necessarily universal for the individual. So someone might use a *towards* meta program (see next) to choose a romantic partner but may use an *away-from* meta program to purchase tuna fish. Thus people are not to be considered as meta program "types," as some NLP books suggest. Meta programs are dependent on the context, not the person.

The Key

The key to using Meta Programs for Mind Control is straightforward and simple. You use the meta program that your subject is using for the context you are discussing. Period.

Meta Program: Towards vs. Away-From

When someone says, "I want/don't want to do this because..." what follows will tell you whether they are motivated by *getting* something (a towards meta program) or *avoiding* something (an away- from meta program).

Consider this, depending on the context and situation, each of us are motivated either by wanting to avoid something that is displeasing or to get something that we desire.

You can very quickly determine someone's towards/away-from meta program by asking, "What's important to you in a ...?"

Meta Program: Options vs. Procedures

When given the choice of how to do something, people will have two ways of responding. They will choose to respond by choosing a set procedure or by deciding among a variety of options. People tending toward procedures will tend to have a set way of doing things. They don't need much for motivation, only a process that they can refer to and rely on.

Those who tend toward options will always be looking for a

better way to do things and love responding creatively with new ideas.

As an example, when you ask, "How did you choose your current job?" an *options* response will sound like this, "I wanted to be in a position that gave me a chance to travel. I looked at my choices and started at the top of my list of most favorite possible jobs and went down the list until I got one."

A *procedures* response will be very systematic and procedural! Something like this, "I went to my friend, and he told me about all the work that flight attendants do, so I read up on it and talked to a few people. One of them used to work as an attendant and told me where to apply, so I looked at some of the trainings and..." This type of story can go for a while.

Using this meta program for Mind Control means that, for a person who tends toward *options* will respond favorably to a presentation that gives them choices, while someone who relies on *procedure* must tell a story.

Meta Program: Relationship (Sameness vs. Difference)

This Meta Program helps determine how much similarities and difference contribute to people's choices.

When asked, "What is the relationship between the (service or product) you want and what you have now?" the subject will respond by either saying that it is *similar* or *different*. There is a common test that NLP practitioners use, in which they show three coins - two heads, one tails.

The subject is bound to answer one of four ways.

"They are all the same. They're all coins."
"They're all different coins."
"They're all the same, except one is tails."
"They're all different, except for they are coins."

When this question is asked about whatever the controller is trying to offer, the controller would tailor the information to the subject's relationship meta program.

In other words, if the subject was asked the relationship between his present car and an ideal car, and he responded that it had to be completely different, then the controller would emphasize the *difference* of the car he's offering, even if he is offering a very similar car.

Likewise, if the subject wants a similar fill-in-the-blank, the controller would point out the *similarities* of what he is offering, even if it is very different.

The exceptions to this:

"They're all the same, except one is tails."

"They're all different, except for they are coins."

You will notice that the subject is pointing out an exception to "all the same" and "all different." In this case, the controller would also give an exception, thus matching the subject's Meta Program.

Convincer Meta Program and Strategy

The convincer strategy starts by asking the subject, "How do you know (product/service) is good?"

The subject will answer one of four ways:

* see it
* read about it
* hear about it from someone
* have it or work with it

The subject's answer will determine whether the controller will show the product/service, give written information, have people tell the subject or have the subject work with that product/service.

The second factor that will ensure the subject is convinced the product/service is good is *time*.

The time factor is elicited by asking the question, "How much time or for how long do you have to see it/read about it/hear about it/work with it?"

That question will fall into four answers:

* once
* x number of times
* specific length of time
* never

If the answer to this second question is *once,* all the controller must do is show, give written material, have someone give a testimonial or have it work with the product or service. Doing this once will be enough.

If the subjects answer is more than once, the controller simply must show, give written material, have someone give a testimonial or have him work with the product or service that number of times.

If the answer is a specific length of time, the controller will show, give written material, have someone give a testimonial or have it work with the product or service, for that length of time. A long length of time can be dealt with by waiting about 20% of that time and saying something to the effect of, "It seems like it has been (name length of time) since we last spoke."

For those people who are never convinced or have to be convinced every time, a different strategy is needed. In this case, hypnotic language patterns are needed.

The controller would first elicit and anchor the certainty that the product/service is good for one time, then say, "Can you imagine feeling that (fire anchor) every time you just think about the product/service, so you don't have to worry about it again?"

Final Note on Meta Programs

There are numerous Meta Programs to consider and think about. This is by no means an in-depth survey of the topic. You are encouraged to study more on the subject. There are a lot of resources available.

Belief Change Processes

NLP is a particularly good therapeutic tool to assist people to reevaluate beliefs that have held them back from accomplishing their goals. Because NLP is often used as a covert tool of persuasion, it can be used to covertly change people's beliefs for Mind Control purposes.

To understand the belief change process, it is easiest to see how it is used in an overt therapeutic setting.

In a therapeutic example, the subject reports that they are hesitant about going to back to school, because they believe they are too old to restart their education.

Here sub-modalities are used, and four different images are elicited and followed by the NLP process that will create the change they needed.

Step 1. The subject is asked to make an image of the belief, "I'm too old to learn," and then is asked the sub-modalities of that image - the location, distance, color/black&white, in motion or still, etc. The NLP practitioner/controller makes notes of these.

Step 2. The subject is then asked to envision a new positive belief that would benefit them, such as "I can learn at any age," and the same sub-modalities are elicited.

Step 3. The same is done for the "something that used to be true but is no longer true." This should be something mundane that has no emotional content.

Step 4. The last image that's elicited is of something that the subject knows is true.

Step 5. The subject is asked then to swiftly move the image of the belief, "I'm too old to learn," into the location of "something that used to be true but is no longer true," and make certain it takes on all the related sub-modalities of "something that used to be true but is no longer true."

Step 6. The image of the belief, "I can learn at any age" is then very quickly moved to the location of "something that is true."

Step 7. The subject is then asked to rehearse seeing these changes. When done well, the belief is permanent.

Covert Belief Change

Changing a belief covertly is a bit trickier, because it requires a great deal of rapport and becoming very skilled with anchoring. To do it covertly, the controller would do the same process as mentioned above, but incorporate covert anchors.

The first step for the controller is to elicit the thing that used to be true, or it could be a thing they know as "wrong." Then fire the anchor, when the discussion turns to their current belief that the controller wants to remove.

The next anchor is for something they know is true and to fire that when the discussion turns to the belief the controller wants to be accepted.

This process is done on a regular basis in many TV commercials.

Additional Belief Change Methods

Simple operant conditioning (see behavioral conditioning) will also work. Reward any movement that is indicative of the new belief and give the cold stare to opposing beliefs.

Using slight of mouth is also effective at combating an existing belief (see Gaslighting).

Another method is to use the voice, where any reference to the old belief is referred to in a whining tone, sarcasm or with some contempt. As a warning, strong rapport is very important, because it can very easily be taken as an insult.

Timeline and Time Manipulation

Timeline refers to how people tend to perceive time as a linear series of events, with events of the past leading to present events, followed by future events. This effect can be drawn as a line in two dimensions.

To figure this out, tell someone to assume that they are standing on a line of time, and ask them where they perceive the past, and have them point to it. Then have them point to their future. With that information, you will understand how they perceive their past and their future.

A controller can elicit a person's timeline, or it can be suggested by a simple use of gestures; the right hand extended to the side can represent the future, and the left hand extended can represent the past. The center is the present.

All of this can be done covertly by talking about the past while extending the left hand, and the future, while extending the right hand. To suggest a future response, the controller can simply gesture to the future and suggest the feeling be there.

Time Manipulation refers to the process of covertly suggesting that a response or feeling from the subject will happen in the future. It can also be used to help the subject imagine a feeling, or even an event, that has happened in the past.

An example of that would be to elicit a feeling and through use of language patterns (mentioned below) to suggest it in the future.

"It is interesting to feel that excitement *tomorrow now,* isn't it?" Note that the time is ambiguous. Is it referring to feeling the excitement now or tomorrow? Because it is ambiguous, BOTH meanings are accepted as true.

Likewise, you can suggest a feeling or response that has happened in the past.

"That excitement you *are* feeling is a great feeling, *wasn't* it?"

Language Patterns

Language patterns are phrases, stories and metaphors combined with other NLP practices (like anchoring and embedded commands) that are designed to covertly elicit a response from the listener. The response desired is usually something emotional, so that it can be anchored in some way.

Language patterns are a unique form of covert hypnotic suggestion. In traditional hypnosis, the hypnotist will give direct suggestions, telling the subject what to do and how to respond. Language patterns differ from traditional hypnotic suggestions in that they are not direct. Instead, the operator often describes a process. In order for the subject who is listening to the pattern to understand the process, they have to go through the process in their mind, doing it to themselves.

The popularity of covert language patterns evolved from NLP practitioners, who wanted to get laid. Then they were packaged into "get laid" NLP products and seminars designed for consumption by the horny male masses, too busy to take an NLP course and figure it out for themselves.

If one can control the emotions of others, they are very likely to follow suggestions. This is because people almost universally make their decisions based on emotion, more than reason. Using emotions, a nation can be driven to war or to build giant monuments. Individuals in a one-on-one are no different; and because a controller can get instant feedback, the control is often easier.

When using language patterns, rapport is *essential*.

Most people who learn language patterns begin first by memorizing existing patterns and, if they're smart, practice them. After some practice, most people start to understand the theory behind language patterns and can begin to generate language patterns on their own.

The I-You Shift

This is a very simple pattern and something that we do all the time in regular conversation.

The I-You shift happens when one begins talking about their experience and instead of using the first person "I" - they shift to "you." This is a covert way of telling someone to feel what you want them to describe.

I was thinking about what happened to me yesterday. I was standing in line at the checkout counter, and someone asked me to hand them a magazine by the register. You know what it is like when someone looks at you and has such a kind voice and manner, that you smile and just do what this person says. And they just smile and tilt their head. It leaves you with such a warm feeling, that you know it is something that you are going to remember for that day.

In this example, using the I-You shift, the speaker is covertly telling the subject to feel a warm feeling toward them.

The Connection Pattern

This one you will recognize from earlier. It is designed to create a sense of connection and familiarity.

I don't know what it is that causes most people to ...notice that feeling of connectedness... to each other. One of my friends was telling me that when she can ...feel that connection... it is like there is this cord of light that connects us (gesture by moving the hand between you and the other person, simulating the connection), and this cord grows with the warmth of that connection. I imagine that it is like you ...feel this "click"... and you can ...see yourself years from now... and still ...feel that connection... and then ...remember back to today... as the start of it. And you can ...feel that right here... (touch the solar plexus of the other person).

Fascination Pattern

This pattern is, as it describes, designed to create fascination.

Have you ever seen something that really got your attention? Maybe it was something you wanted... to buy... or a maybe you got in a conversation that could really... **grab your attention**... *it is like whatever you have right in front of you is the only thing ...**that's in your awareness**... and you ... **focus in**... because what you have in front of you is so compelling that you close off everything else... when it is as if you just ... **begin to fall**...into the thought that something... **like this**... can be so compelling that time stops...*

These patterns can go on for as long as the operator cares to describe them.

Here is another attraction pattern.

Isn't it interesting how everyone is so different, yet in so many ways, we are all the same. I mean, for example, I don't know what it is you do, when you decide for yourself that you really want to be with someone, and you know it is what you want, because you find yourself imagining it ... you picture it, and your mine, and you look forward to it, for all the right reasons. Reasons that are right to you, because you know its what you want, but I think you know a person can find that ,when that's what's taking place, Wow, what a difference in the way they think, and just how readily you then begin to make time for this special person you are now connecting so strongly with. Its a totally different experience... its like you feel almost magnetically drawn to this person - you know what I mean? And sometimes, I think a person wouldn't even know that that's what's taking place, until afterward. And you look back on it as one of those amazing memories you treasure/cherish for the rest of your life ... now ... with me, as I think long and hard about it, I think that's the process of discovering that a person is being drawn to another person.

This one is referred to at the BJ Pattern

I was just sitting here thinking about taking a vacation, if you could imagine your ideal vacation spot - what would it be like? (Stop and let her talk).

You know, I think its so interesting how people connect with their hopes and their desires and their daydreams right ... I was reading this article the other day about compulsions, and it got me to thinking about the difference between compulsion and anticipation.

I mean, have you ever come home from a hard day at work, and the boss was a jerk and kept piling the papers up on your desk, and its like all you can think about it is dropping your clothes and getting into that steamy hot bath or shower. That's like before you even step in, you can already feel that heat working its way through every muscle in your body, and all your frustrations just drop away, and all you can feel is the pleasure of that warmth, just shooting through every part of you. And then there is that moment of sliding in, where you really let that pleasure take you, and it just feels great, doesn't it?

Yeah, well do you like chocolate? (Is there a food where when you see it you absolutely have to put it in your mouth?) I mean, can you stop and remember a time when you, it is like you see that piece of chocolate and your mouth is already tasting it before you even put it in. You can already taste that sweetness against your tongue, and you can feel the special rich texture of it against your tongue as well. You know that texture that really good chocolate has. And then there is that moment, that moment when the first molecule of chocolate touches your tongue, and you know it is inside your mouth, and you just want to keep it there, because it is so rich and so good. And there is that extra special warmth, when you swallow that sweetness down.

Or then maybe, you know like sometimes, you meet someone, and you are really attracted to them, and you both know it, and there is that moment when your eyes lock; it is that special look, just before you kiss for the very first time, and you are trembling with anticipation, and your heart is pounding, because you are thinking about how good it is going to be. It is like every physical moment of that relationship is enfolded/contained or rolled into that first touch of the lips, and there is that excitement, with that first soft contact of the lips, where you don't even know if you are touching or not, but then, oh man. It is like a jolt of electricity all through you. See, I think what happens is the conscious mind goes down into the unconscious and brings back up all these thoughts, images, desires and fantasies, and you may think those thoughts are above me, but really I think they're blow me, because you are coming from a much deeper part of your mine, aren't you?

Forbidden Dark Patterns

Dark patterns refer to patterns that can be used to harm. These types of language patterns tend to create depression, fear and guilt. They are the most difficult, because it requires a lot of rapport, combined with stealth and guile. It is like using a velvet glove to hide a steel hammer.

Disclaimer
Neither the author, the publisher nor anyone known to them endorses the use of these patterns.

The Hospital Pattern

This is a fear-inducing pattern that produces a fear of loss. It begins by describing a loss of something of great emotional value.

a) *Did you ever know someone that went into a hospital and never came back?*

b) *It is amazing how often people just go and never come back.*

c) *If you like what we have, remember that I could leave you and never come back.*

The operator would then capture the pieces into a nice little story and likely multiply the effect, using anchors.

Example said to lover:

a) *Did you hear about (insert famous person or acquaintance) who went to the hospital for something (anchor here) and never came out?*

b) *By the way, I had a doggie that I loved, and one day it just disappeared (use same anchor here with more intensity), (keep building value of doggie). She was so good to me, she would wait for me after school. and she would just kiss me and knock me down ever so gently. We would roll on the floor and play all kinds of games.*

c) *We would chase each other; she would fetch for me; she even slept in my room (what could you do with this?) But then one day, I came looking for her, and she wasn't there. You have no idea what it feels like to lose someone like that (anchor). For days, you look for her, you post posters, you post rewards. No matter what you do, it is over, gone, out of your life (anchor).*

The Depression Pattern

This pattern is very advanced, because it employs *values*.

Elicitation & Anchoring

The start of the pattern is to elicit the life values of the subject. In other words, the process begins with rapport and the operator asking, "What's important to you in life?" This will lead the subject finally to reveal whatever those values are and, for this example, let's say the subject answers, "Family, religion and work," in that order of priority.

The operator will then ask the question, "What are you *not* thinking about?" This question will bring about a profound state of confusion in the subject, at which time the operator would covertly anchor the confusion with a touch or gesture.

The operator would then begin to talk about the subject's values of *family*, *religion* and *work*, and fire off the confusion anchor, linking confusion to these values, effectively nullifying them.

Mind Control 101

The most malicious use of this or any "dark" pattern would be to have the subject practice this response and have it effectively predetermined as an outcome. This might sound something like this:

I'm not sure how well you can imagine thinking about family, religion and work, and still having this feeling (firing anchor) in the future...from now on... but that's not something you have to think about consciously, as it takes place.

Consider now why this type of pattern is so malicious. When done effectively, anytime the subject thinks about what they used to have value in - *family*, *religion* and *work*, they now feel confused.

Elements of Dark NLP Patterns

There is an element of some Dark NLP patterns that, in itself, is not bad and is often used to help in an NLP therapeutic setting. It is creating an anchor for "things that used to be true."

The hypnotic version of this would be to have the subject create a place or even a box in their mind, that they put things that are no longer true for them. They can put habits, compulsions and cravings in the box, so that they are no longer true. The result is very effective and positive for the subject.

But what if the operator has them put things there that they value?

The effect would be much like the previous pattern.

Story Telling as Language Pattern

When anyone tells a story, especially a vivid and compelling story, they are using metaphors to covertly influence and hypnotize.

Because a story is not about the people it is being told to, they can listen without feeling preached at. But in order for them to truly understand the story, they must, at some level, feel the emotions of the characters. This is where story telling is a great tool for Mind Control.

There are several good examples of this that can help a beginner understand the process of Mind Control. The first example is fairly common and happens any time someone reads a story or watches a movie and becomes so involved in the story line that they forget the fact they are involving themselves in a fiction.

In spite of the fact that they are maybe sitting on their couch reading or watching a TV show, they react as if they are in the story.

Mind Control 101

In other words, they are being affected by what they are reading/watching *as if it were real.*

This has been used by Mind Controllers all throughout history, and many shamanic cultures place the story teller as the central person in their rituals.

To learn this skill, it is best that the controller first go into their history and remember times when they were reading or watching a show and got so intensely involved that they lost track of time and began to care about the characters in the story.

What was it that made it so interesting?

How was it you forgot where you were at and 'got into the story'?

What emotions did the story involve?

By answering these questions, the controller can begin to understand what kinds of stories move them, and begin to craft stories they can tell that are equally involving.

How does one craft a story that delivers a covert message? There are a few factors that one needs to consider and try to incorporate.

1. Tell a story with a character that is similar to the listener. The main character needs to have something that the listener can relate to, regardless if the main character is a turtle or a human being.

2. If telling the story orally (aloud), become involved yourself. The more passion, energy and enthusiasm you can put in the story, the more the audience will react to it.

3. Lead off the subject at times. The more convoluted a story becomes, the more the listener must involve themselves to follow it. Often you will hear a story begin like this:

When I was little boy, my mother would send me over to her mother's house, my grandmother, and she would tell me stories from the old country. I've never heard these stories, except from here, so I don't know if she made them up or if they're just part of the folklore. She told me that when she was a little girl, her cousin would tease her to go to the "The Witch's House" and talk to the lady they called "The Witch." The thing was that the witch didn't mind being called that ,and my grandmother always approached the house scared, and every time the Witch would befriend her, take her in, tell her a story, and she'd leave always feeling better. Her friends told her that The Witch put a spell on her, which scared her every time; yet she would still go back for more.

Well, one day The Witch told her a story about when she was a little girl and how she was always concerned about getting too close to the Black Lake. The Black Lake, they told her, was haunted and would pull young girls in from the shore and drown them, if they didn't take a certain path to the shore....

Just from this introduction, it is hard to tell who the story is really about - the person telling the story, the grandmother, The Witch?

In order to understand it, the listener must forget who the story is about and follow deeper and deeper into the story, eventually losing themselves it in.

4) Design a message in the story. The message in the story can be like a moral of the story, like Aesop's Fables. The message can also be much more covert. The covert message is one of emotion, meaning there is an emotion that the main character feels that motivates them. This emotion must be justified in the story. In doing this, the subject that hears the story can relate to the emotion.

Exercise:

Make up and tell a story that is convoluted, like the one above. Write it down if you have to. Observe how they respond. If you get a glassy-eyed stare in the midst of telling it, that is a sign of a hypnotic state induced by the story.

Other Variations of Story Telling

A testimonial is another example of story telling, because it is one person saying what happened to them with a certain product or service. It is used everywhere, from the religious practice of "witnessing" to TV commercials featuring both stars and ordinary people telling their story.

Exercise:

Make a list of all the times a testimonial has been used to sell a product or promote a service. Consider how you can do that with your outcome in mind. Who can tell the story? What will they say?

The Voice Roll

The voice roll is a way of speaking that is very common among public speakers and especially common with preachers giving sermons.

The voice roll is a way of speaking that has specific rhythm. The rhythm creates a hypnotic effect with a majority of the audience. The reason why is that the rhythm itself becomes unconsciously anticipated, and thus the listener follows the rhythm.

The specifics of the rhythm is about pausing briefly, 45 to 60 times a minute, or about once a second.

Here is an example of the voice roll with (...) representing the brief pause:

There is pattern... of unique thinking ... that allows us... to see how each of us... can create such power... create such influence... that people will follow.... Now... think of it!.... It is all in how you think... that propels others... to follow.... It is as if you have behind you... a force of will... and that's what it is... a force of Will!! So think about what you want... Think about how... you want to effect people... Imagine that you CAN... and you are on your way...

Another way of setting a rhythm is to pace it according to the breath, breathing normally and only speaking on the exhale. This creates a unique pattern that is unconscious. To understand it, consider what happens when we breathe with emotion. When we feel excitement, the emphasis is on the exhale. We sigh with relief. By pausing on the inhale, the speaker is stimulating the part of the unconscious mind that inhales with anticipation, and by speaking on the exhale, unconsciously providing relief.

When speaking to an individual, the speaker would pace the breathing of the listener. Speaking to a group is much easier, as the speaker does not have to pace anyone. The process alone will allow the audience to follow the inhale-exhale/anticipation-relief pattern.

Exercise

Take a book, and before reading aloud, notice your breath. Breathe the same way as you read aloud, only speaking on the exhale.

Eye Accessing Cues

Eye accessing cues describe a particular way that we tend to be hardwired. This is a tendency and not to be taken as a hard and fast rule.

Eye accessing cues show that, when people are thinking in a

certain way, their eyes tend to move in a particular direction.

There are several cop shows on TV that show a police interrogation, in which the police determine a suspect is lying, simply by watching the movement of their eyes and knowing about eye accessing cues.

The first time "Visual Accessing Cues" were discussed was by Richard Bandler and John Grinder in their book "Frogs into Princes: Neuro Linguistic Programming (NLP). " From their experiments, they found that the following applies, when a question was asked to "normally organized," right-handed people.

Keep in mind that right-left is determined from your viewpoint, looking at them.

* When the eyes look up and to the left, this indicates "Visually Constructed," meaning they are having to make pictures in their head.

Example: Ask someone to make a picture of a red hippopotamus wearing a blue tutu, and watch their eyes.

* When the eyes look up and to the right, it indicates "Visual Remembered," meaning the image is a memory

Example: Ask someone the color of their mother's hair, and watch their eyes.

These two examples are often used as the lie detector in cop shows. The cop would ask the suspect to describe what happened at the time a crime occurred. If they looked up and to the left, they were remembering the event. If the suspect looked up and to the right, they were constructing the event and not remembering it. In other words, they were lying.

What about the other eye movements?

* When someone is looking to the left, they are usually in an "Auditorily Constructed" mode, meaning they are making noises or dialogs in their mind. One can notice this when asking someone, "Imagine Darth Vader's voice whispering your name with a lisp."

* When someone is looking to the right, it is an indication of an "Auditorily Remembered" thought, meaning they are recalling the sound of something. Think of your favorite song, and imagine it in your mind.

* When someone is looking down and to the left ,they tend to

access an emotion or feeling. One can notice this by asking someone to remember an emotion.

* When someone is looking down and to the right, it means that they are talking to themselves.

It would be a mistake to treat this as a hard and fast rule. People will vary. Left-handed people will tend to be the exact opposite of the above eye accessing model, and some people will not conform to this model. The solution is flexibility and sensory acuity.

There is a very simple exercise and a fun game that anyone can use to gain the skill of eye accessing cues.

Exercise:

Take a few friends and ask them to tell you four things, and have one of them be a lie. With a little practice, you will be able to determine each person's lying eye accessing cues. Teach them the skill, if you like to make it more fun.

NLP for Group Presentations

For a public speaker, there exists a very special opportunity to evoke the powers of Mind Control, when speaking to a group.

When speaking to a group, the group has made an unspoken agreement among the group members to listen and follow the speaker. To be a good public speaker, Mind Control is not just an option, it is an obligation.

There are several beliefs, assumptions, specific actions and skills that a public speaker can use to gain control over the mind of the group.

Belief: Public Speaking is Fun, Easy

This is a common belief among those who are good public speakers, who can move a crowd.

There are two things that anyone can do to gain this belief. The first is simply by doing the NLP belief change processes on themselves, that were mentioned earlier.

The second thing is to create as many opportunities to speak in public as possible.

"The more you sweat in training, the less you bleed in combat."
~ Anonymous, U.S. Special Forces

With practice, the skill of public speaking can be learned and utilized as a wonderful tool of Mind Control.

Mind Control 101

Assumption: People are here to get my information and want to be led

This assumption/belief is basically true for any public speech or presentation. Whether it is a political rally, theatrical play, religious sermon, college pep rally, lecture or seminar, people are there to fulfill two criteria: to get information and to react to what they hear (i.e., to be led).

This assumption on the part of the speaker gives them the permission to do whatever they can to hold the audience's attention, while delivering their message.

Conviction: Belief in the Product

When a public speaker believes in what they are speaking about, they become impassioned. That energy is conveyed to the audience during the delivery and should be amplified.

It has been said that an audience will only respond to about 10% of the speaker's energy. For that reason, many public speakers make their presentations "hyper" and sometimes even *manic*. This can be very effective, when the speaker has developed rapport with the crowd. Gaining rapport with the group will be discussed in the section "Unifying the Group Through Group Action."

By combining the assumption that people are present to be led and the deep conviction in your product or service, a public speaker can do a great deal of "pacing and dragging" of an audience.

Attitude: Magnanimity (aka Charisma):

"They care about me, and I care about them."

While many people talk about the power of charisma, few will describe how to develop it. For that reason, it is better to focus on a more specific and measurable quality - *magnanimity*.

Magnanimity is the act of being liked and appreciated. It also has the same feeling of liking and appreciation toward those doing the liking. Combine magnanimity with the qualities of *conviction* and *belief* that public speaking is fun and easy, and a very powerful mental state is created for public speaking. A controller can use the belief changing processes mentioned earlier to get into this state.

With this knowledge, the controller in the public speaking setting looks at everyone in the audience and the audience as a whole, as if they are each best friends and that these friends are eager to hear and be with the controller.

Speaking to the "Group Mind"

For someone speaking to a group, it is impractical to think in terms of controlling every individual within the group. There are simply too many minds there to deal with to effectively influence every one of them. In theory, however, there is a synergy created by all those minds coming together in the same place. It is called "The Group Mind." The goal of any public speaker is to use all their tools to direct the Group Mind.

In reality, "The Group Mind" is a metaphor to help us understand how a group functions as a unit.

There are certain things that can be assumed about the group mind. As a synergy of all the minds in the group, the Group Mind is easily distracted and generally passive, unless incited. It is the responsibility of the speaker to harness and direct the attention of the Group Mind.

One technique used is a mental/self-hypnotic process used by the controller on him/herself. This is a metaphoric mental construct used to gather energy from the Group Mind for the presentation and to direct it.

The controller envisions a "group mind" that floats above the group, perhaps as a brain or a ball of energy. Each individual in the group is connected to the group mind by invisible tentacles, which the controller also imagines.

The next step is to tap into the energy of the group mind. This is done by envisioning a conveyor belt or conduit that goes from the group mind directly to the speaker.

Two additional processes are added to this mental exercise. Before the energy connects with the speaker, a "converter" is installed to turn all the energy into positive energy. Then an amplifier increases the energy, before it reaches the speaker.

The speaker then imagines that the energy is projected back to the individual audience members, as she/he speaks through the speaker's voice and the eyes.

The cycle continues, with the audience's energy increased and fed again into the group mind, continuing in an endless loop.

For the speaker who incorporates this metaphoric process, the result of this is that it energizes both the speaker and the audience. Some speakers have reported a "high" after giving a presentation using this technique. This is very important, because the audience as a whole will only get about 10% of the enthusiasm that the speaker projects, so the more energy/enthusiasm from the speaker, the more affected the group mind.

Tactic: Unifying the Group Through Group Action

A very skilled public speaker knows that if the group is unified, they are easier to control, as a group. The way to do that in the most physical way is to have them do something as a group. The best modern example of that is the "stadium wave." If you are not familiar with the stadium wave, it occurs in sports areas when a group of spectators stand with hands raised, then sit down. They are followed by the people next to them doing the same. When the wave begins, everyone eagerly anticipates their chance to join in, and in doing so, the group unifies.

In a lecture or seminar, the speaker can create the same sense of unity, by introducing a group exercise, in which everyone must participate.

An example of this is having everyone stand up and stretch and asking the members of the group to introduce themselves to each other - but keep in mind that any exercise that involves the entire group will work.

Keeping the group unified is done by doing these exercises on a regular basis.

Tactic: Elicitation for Groups

Eliciting emotions and mental states from a group is different from working with individuals. The group itself does not have a way of communicating a pre-existing group emotion or state, so instead, the emotion or state is suggested, and the individuals in the group are asked to model the emotion or state.

As an example, let's take the emotion of wanton desire and anticipation. The speaker would begin to describe the emotion/state:

We've all had the feeling of wanting something... that feeling of ... when you think about what you want... you've just gotta have it ... and how the longer you wait, the more you want it... and then there comes that time when you realize you are going to get it... and there is this wonderful eager feeling... anticipation... like when you are on the start of a roller coaster and it is going up... building... more and more...Do you remember that feeling?"

Let's talk about what makes something interesting. Everyone knows what it is like to have something that is so interesting... so compelling that you can't turn away... and you lock in... like it is right in front of you...and it takes up all your field of vision... it is compelling, and all you want is to know more.... That's the interest I want you to remember.

When the speaker delivers this with energy (i.e. enthusiasm), it will have an impact on the Group Mind and impart a percentage of that emotion.

Tactic: Linking Emotions to the Speaker

This is much easier than it might first appear. Consider that the speaker has the attention of the audience and can introduce any subject. Typically, this is done is by creating a pretense to discuss a dichotomy of emotions and having the audience look up at the speaker.

Example:

To really get the most from this training, we're going to discuss trust and how it effects each of us. Take a moment to close your eyes, and remember a time when you lost trust. Remember what it is like to lose trust. Now, open your eyes, and discuss the feeling. (pause) Now remember the feeling of trust. Close your eyes, and bring about that feeling of trust. Remember that feeling, and bring it about. Feel it. Now, open your eyes, and look up here.

In this case, the speaker is covertly creating the feeling of trust and, by having the audience look at him, link that trust to him.

Any emotion can be linked to the speaker in this way. In fact, there are several trainers who use this extremely well during a seminar. Once they know the audience is following them, they will use the procedure to link wisdom, trust, awe, amazement, joy to themselves.

Strategy: Using Conflict to Unify the Group
Hecklers and Controversy

While most people will think that conflict within a group is a divisive quality, a good speaker will use it as a tool to bring the group into unity.

One way a speaker can do this is to introduce controversy very early into the presentation. This can be done by openly and unapologetically mentioning the criticisms and conflicts that others have toward the topic being discussed. Starting off by saying, "This is very controversial, because..." is enough. This creates a tension in the minds of anyone listening, that they are being let in on a topic that others criticize and that the speaker is open and honest enough to address this right from the start .

When a member of the group challenges the speaker, many speakers would find this a challenge. A skilled speaker interested in Mind Control will consider it an opportunity. This is important, because the norm of the group is one of equilibrium and stasis, and any challenge to the leader disrupts that status quo and brings the group closer.

Dealing with the heckler is important, and various skills, like embedded commands, can be done so that the commands are addressed directly to the heckler.

Tactic: Telling a Story

(See "Story Telling as Language Pattern"). This will never get old. People have been sitting down to be led by a good story, ever since humans could talk around a campfire, and they continue to do it with the technology of television today.

Many skilled public speakers will make a point to tell a long, involved story that drags the audience though a long list of emotions, often ending with something that is inspiring and tearful. It is often then that they pitch their product or ask for a donation.

When using story telling, one tactic they often employ is to not warn the audience that they are going to tell the story. They just begin, and let it go... the audience has no way of resisting.

Use of Language Pattens

Just like story telling, public speaking is an ideal venue for using language patterns. In fact, a good public speaker will use language patterns in their presentation, and they often do it unconsciously, as a result of a lot of experience. The moral - get a lot of experience speaking in public.

Anchoring the group

A public speaker can use what is called "spacial anchoring" to elicit emotional responses from the audience. This is done by using the gestures and the location on the stage where the speaker is standing.

For example, the speaker can elicit through metaphor the feelings of want, desire and "go for it," when standing in a specific spot on the stage. When the speaker wants the audience to buy a product or make a donation, he'll return to that particular spot, while talking about the product or requesting a donation.

How to Get Started at Group Mind Control

There are endless opportunities to do public speaking and practice these skills. You can start locally by calling up any of your public service organizations, like Optimists Club, Kiwanis Club, Rotary Club, Lions Club and the list goes on. Just call up your local Chamber of Commerce, and ask for a list of these groups.

When calling the group, pick a topic that you are interested in. You won't be paid, but most of these groups gather for a lunch or dinner meeting, so the benefit is you will get a free meal. When you do a lot of them, you will learn why it is called the "rubber chicken circuit." Don't worry about impressing them. if this is your first time; they are used to sitting through some very boring presentations, and yours will likely be better than most.

Hypnosis

Hypnosis is one of the oldest forms of documented Mind Control in history. In spite of all the books and training about hypnosis that are available, hypnosis is much easier and simpler than anyone wants you to believe.

Most hypnotists rely on two crutches that in practical terms serve only to perpetuate the belief that hypnosis is hard. They are the "pre-talk" and "progressive relaxation induction."

The pre-talk is usually a long monologue that a hypnotist will give the subject, so that they'll understand what's going to happen, and follow instructions.

The progressive relaxation induction is a way to induce

hypnosis, by instructing the subject to relax, usually starting at one end of the body and going over the entire body, one body part at a time. It is a very long and monotonous process that, for some hypnotists, is the only process they know. It is also an incredible waste of time.

Both the pre-talk and the progressive relaxation induction can be avoided and lots of time saved.

The solution to both of these are rapport and giving a simple instruction. It goes like this, "All I want you to do is simply follow my instructions. Don't analyze or judge what you hear. Just make it true for you, as if it were your reality. Do you agree?"

The hypnotist then waits for them to agree, and then it is done. From there, the hypnotist gives a series of instructions that convince the subject that they are hypnotized, and then teach them how to do incredible things and have wonderful feelings using hypnosis.

Here is the an example of the hypnotic process:

All I want you to do is simply follow my instructions. Don't analyze or judge what you hear. Just make it true for you, as if it were your reality. Agreed? (wait for response).

Close your eyes, and command the eyes to "Stay Closed!" and imagine them sealed tightly closed... so tightly closed that no one could open them... so tightly closed that even you could not open them. Make that so!.... and when you have ... prove it to yourself, and test it. Make it so! The eyelids stay closed. So stop testing. The reason they stay closed is that you followed the instructions, and you are a very good hypnosis subject. Now, relax and go deeper.

Then a whole series of instructions are given and tested. These tests can be for deeper relaxation, catalepsy (inability to move), to create pleasant feelings, amnesia, to various degrees up to forgetting major information like their name, carrying out suggestions in the hypnotic state and so on.

With the passing of each test, the subject is congratulated (positive feedback) so that the subject knows how to correctly follow hypnotic instructions.

As the process continues, the subject goes through the process of hypnotic conditioning, where they learn to respond to commands automatically.

Mind Control 101

Not every subject will respond quickly, and some will require more training than others.

A very thorough description of hypnotic conditioning can be found in my book, *Perfected Mind Control: The Unauthorized Black Book of Hypnotic Mind Control*.

Subliminal Suggestions

There are many ways to deliver subliminal suggestions. Most commonly known is the urban myth of words, "Drink Coke!" and "Eat Popcorn!" which were allegedly flashed on the screen of a movie. This story has been very difficult to verify, but it has been reported as increasing sales. It was alleged that these messages were repeatedly flashed at less than a fifth of a second, just outside the human ability to consciously be aware of it.

Let's assume this myth is true and based in fact. The fact that the viewer has no reason to suspect that these messages are being displayed is central to its success. If they were told that the film is full of subliminal messages, it is likely that they would begin to notice the messages and consciously resist them.

This last point is a reminder that *people can't resist what they can't detect.*

Doing this on a large scale, for the purpose of Mind Control, has some technical obstacles to overcome. With current technology of video editing, it is possible to create video presentations that flash or overlay messages or images in this manner.

A second factor in using this form of subliminal messaging is frequency. Only by flashing these messages repeatedly will the unconscious mind recognize the pattern, and then follow the suggestions.

In recent years, there have been new spam emails to buy products that contain a quick flash of the word, "Buy!"

The effectiveness of these subliminal messages have yet to tested with any scientific scrutiny. With that said, subliminal messages, theoretically, should impact the mind.

The evidence of that is mostly testimonial; for example, embedded commands (mentioned earlier) have a long history of delivering messages that impress the user at the results they receive.

One way of using embedded commands on a large scale would

be to have a pre-recorded message played over loud speakers as a regular public service announcement:

Hello shoppers, buy now! You can see all the great bargains we offer at SpendMart. Making sure you feel satisfied with your choices is our job. As you shop here at SpendMart, feel free to ask for your discount card, and keep shopping to find your best deal. And thanks for shopping!

There are various ways to do the same thing with visual media. One way to do this is the controller considers the desired outcome and places items, pictures and decorations in the areas that the subjects would see. These items, on the most obvious level, appear to be nothing out of the ordinary; however, within the items can be hidden images and words that 1) directly state the outcome, like "trust" or 2) imply it through imagery.

Fast Talking to Deliver Subliminal Messages

After gaining rapport, a controller can be telling stories or lecturing. When the words begin to flow quickly, very short, fast commands can be delivered, and as long as the story continues at a rapid pace, the commands will quickly be ignored; in other words, they go directly to the unconscious mind. Because the commands are not relevant to the story, the secret is to not mark them off, like embedded commands. Example:

This was one of the best pieces of real estate that I've got listed get real excited in this location. There is a hot tub and outdoor pool in the back. Let me show it to you really feel at home. Over here is the kitchen; it's complete with new fridge and fully stocked can't wait to see the upstairs, the pantry could keep you stocked for a year.

Using Ambiguities as Subliminal Messaging

Another way of delivering subliminal messages is through the use of linguistic ambiguities. These ambiguities bypass the listeners conscious awareness, because the sentences don't fit into an understandable linguistic construct, and it is simply "not heard."

As an example, read this sentence aloud, "You can either say 'Yes, I want it' or 'No that this is the right thing to do."

In this case, the "no" is an ambiguity for "know." While this may seem very awkward, using it is even more interesting, because people don't notice!

Take this example of a linguistic ambiguity:

"Here is a product that you might want to take a look at it with excitement."

You will notice that there are almost two sentences there. The first "Here is a product that you might want to take a look at" and "Look at it with excitement."

Ambiguities work, because there are two or more meanings that one can get from the sentence, so the unconscious mind accepts both meanings, while the conscious mind only recognizes the one that makes the most sense.

Here are examples of other ambiguities:

"I'm sure you will find this an interesting experience this as something powerful."

"Please, get behind the wheel and take it for a drive yourself to wanting it really is a good car."

"The choice is all yours. You can say 'Yes' you want it or you can say 'No' (know) that it is the right thing to do."

Psychic Cold Readings

Cold Reading refers to the act of telling things about someone, in such away that it appears to come from "psychic" influences.

There is nothing psychic about psychic cold reading. It is strictly a skill that combines very generalized statements that most people will agree to; the ability to read people at a glance; and a few tricks of guile.

Doing psychic cold readings exercises a particular mental muscle that is absolutely essential for Mind Control - thinking on "a higher level."

To explain this, consider how the higher up the levels of power you go, the more you control. The same is true of knowledge; the more you can know, the more you can influence.

Psychic readings require the reader to quickly observe someone, and make global assumptions about them. The psychic reader gathers more information from their observation than the normal person, just by paying attention. From that, the reader finds an artful way to describe what they've learned from their quick scan, and do it in such a way that the subject feels as if someone is reading their diary.

Being able to do a psychic reading creates an opportunity for any controller to meet and speak with anyone who shows an interest. Simply by saying, "You have very nice energy. Do you have a spiritual practice?" can quickly lead to doing a psychic cold reading.

In a social setting or party, people will quickly find a way to talk to the psychic in the room.

Before going any further, it is important to point out that this attempt at describing psychic cold reading is not to discredit those people who truly feel they are psychic. This is merely a description of the psychic cold reading process.

What are the Basic Rules of Cold Reading?

1. Never refer to what you are doing as a "trick." This undermines the mysteriousness of what you are doing and can turn you into a trickster, instead of someone that people want to learn from.

2. If you resort to some form of slight of hand or magic during the reading, under no circumstances reveal how it was done.

3. Practice. Practice as much as you can, with as many people as possible. The more you practice, the better you will get at reading people and being able to "talk on your feet," as if you were a psychic.

4. If you do use magic tricks during your psychic presentation, use them sparingly and only to add impact to your presentation. Never do more than three or four, unless you are getting paid for your psychic reading.

5. Don't tell the reader anything directly. Instead, you can use anything like the following statements, "I feel..." "My intuition tells me..." "The sense I get is that..."

6. Bill yourself as doing it only for entertainment, but make your presentation as serious as possible.

7. Some cold reading books would tell you, for ethical reasons, that you should never claim supernatural powers. That does not forbid you from allowing people to think it. In fact, people will believe it more, if they conclude it on their own, without any explicit instructions. You can even make it more convincing, by trying to persuade them not to tell anyone.

So what does a non-psychic cold reader use to convince people of their psychic powers?

The first tool is sensory acuity and being a good observer. With experience and a bit of study, anyone can learn how to read someone, based on their age, dress, posture, jewelery, hair style and how they interact with people. Based on this information, the reader makes opening statements and intersperses them with statements that are likely to be true.

Some of these clues are:

* People who wear their watch on the right wrist are likely left-handed. The reader can say, "You grew up knowing that something was different, and you tried hard to fit in. You notice how a lot of people are conformists and how you are different."

* Red-headed people, especially with curly hair and freckles, will find the following statement generally true, "I can tell that, for you, there was some trouble you had with people seeing you as being different; you even got a bit of teasing when you were younger. Eventually, what you found is that you had to find a balance between being different, to meet their expectations, and then deciding that what they thought was not your concern."

* People, especially women, who wear a lot of jewelry (and make-up) will be very likely to find this statement true for them, "There is a concern that you try to hide about how people perceive you. You want to always create a positive first impression, because you know how important it is, and it will allow you to more easily reveal that part of you that is deeper... the part of you that has more depth and is not so easily seen at first glance."

* During a reading, people may be rapt by what you say, with eyes locked on you, or their eyes will be darting back and forth, trying to find out, internally, if your statements are true for them. In this latter case, and with people who are more skeptical, the following statement can be used, "You don't always take things at face value. You make a point of testing out what people tell you as fact."

* Very attractive women will often find this statement true, "You have a habit of attracting the wrong type of man." and "Even though you are often told that you are attractive, you find that you are your

own worst critic; never truly satisfied with what you have and always looking for some area that might need improvement."

As an exercise, begin to make a list and collect your own list of these statements - and *practice, practice and practice.*

Good Generalized Statements that Most People will Agree Applies to Them
The Forer Effect

The Forer Effect is a psychological phenomenon described by Bertam Forer in 1949. The Forer Effect occurs when a very general statement is said to describe someone's personality, and the person will most often agree that it is true, remembering the statements that are favorable and accurate and dismissing and forgetting those statements that are inaccurate. This selectiveness of the human mind allows the person receiving the psychic reading to retrofit the information, in order to accept it as true.

For example, Forer gave a personality test to people, and each person was given the same personality description below. When read, most people agreed that it was an accurate description of their personality.

> *Some of your aspirations tend to be pretty unrealistic. At times, you are extroverted, affable, sociable, while at other times you are introverted and reserved. You have found it unwise to be too frank in revealing yourself to others. You pride yourself on being an independent thinker and do not accept others opinions, without satisfactory proof. You prefer a certain amount of change and variety; you become dissatisfied, when hemmed in by restrictions and limitations. At times, you have serious doubts as to whether you have made the right decision or done the right thing. Disciplined and controlled on the outside, you tend to be worrisome and insecure on the inside.*
>
> *Your sexual adjustment has presented some problems for you. While you have some personality weaknesses, you are generally able to compensate for them. You have a great deal of unused capacity, which you have not turned to your advantage. You have a tendency to be*

critical of yourself. You have a strong need for other people to like you and for them to admire you.

People close to you have been taking advantage of you. Your basic honesty has been getting in your way. Many opportunities that you have had offered to you in the past have had to be surrendered, because you refuse to take advantage of others. You like to read books and articles to improve your mind. In fact, if you are not already in some sort of personal service business, you should be. You have an infinite capacity for understanding people's problems, and you can sympathize with them. But you are firm when confronted with obstinacy or outright stupidity. Law enforcement would be another field you understand. Your sense of justice is quite strong.

Except for the fact that many people wanting a reading also want to hear more than just about their personality, it is possible to give the very same basic reading, by simply having a script that includes these types of statements.

The following is a list of the most common topics that people are interested in during a psychic reading. It would be a good idea to write a list of responses to each of these topics that will apply to most people, and give good, general recommendations:

* Sex
* Spouse (if married)
* Fidelity
* Choice of partner (if single)
* Engagement
* Personal Appearance
* Health
* Physical Activity
* Physical Health
* Health of Other
* Mental Health
* Money
* How money is spent
* Recovery from debts

Mind Control 101

* Career Change
* Gambling Investments
* Property
* Loans

Giving Covert Suggestions During a Psychic Reading

A psychic reading is a great place to give embedded commands and other hypnotic-like suggestions. For example, it is nice to have someone who is responsive to the psychic's reading and is paying attention, so the reader can make that a part of the reading.

You seem like someone who can really... focus in... on something, when it is right in front of you... and you...find it interesting... there are certain things that do get your attention... One of those things is when you have a chance to learn about yourself....

Tricks on Reading People

This effect is so simple that, when I first heard of it, I really didn't think it would do much. It can be used as an opener, but I think it is put to better use a few minutes after meeting a woman and chatting with her. Keep in mind that you can segue into these effects any way you wish. Practice different ways of introducing them to see what suits you best.

Effect: You take her wrists, and tell her to close her eyes, and concentrate on one hand or the other. After a few seconds, you tell her which hand she was thinking about.

How it is done: Take her hands in yours, and then find her pulse on each arm with your thumbs. It may be awkward, at first, from where you're sitting, but what I do is 'follow her thumbs' – put your thumbs at the top of hers, and follow them down, until you hit the pulse. Whichever hand she is concentrating on will have a quicker pulse, so select that one. You can perform this effect more than once with the same person, but I prefer not to.

Understanding Personality Types

A little psychology can go a *long* way, when doing psychic cold readings. Take personality types, for example.

There are plenty of great resources on-line and in books to help anyone learn about personality types and use them in cold readings so this description is by no means in depth. It is just enough to get you headed in the right direction.

There are many different ways of categorizing personalities and any of them will be useful for you. The most common is the Meyers-Briggs Type Indicator that consists of four qualities of personalities that each have two possible choices. These are:

Social Orientation:
    Extrovert(E)
    Introverted(I)

Information Gathering:
    Sensation(S)
    Intuition(N)

Decision Process:
    Thinking(T)
    Feeling(F)

Relationship to the Outside World:
    Judgment(J)
    Perception(P)

By understanding the variations in personalities, a reading can quickly conclude things about people from a very brief observation, which can add huge amounts of content to the reading.

For example, if someone appears reserved and introverted, the following statement will be easy for them to accept as true, "Time with yourself is very important. Even though you have people in your life you interact with, you are most comfortable dealing with your own thoughts and feelings."

An extroverted personality would easily accept this statement as true, "You have a great ability to enjoy the company of others. Sure, there are times when you need to collect your thoughts and be alone, but you can easily devote your time to others and be energized by these interactions."

Tarot Card and Palmistry

Tarot cards and palmistry can be a great resource for a cold reader, because they naturally give the impression of authority. When people see you doing a tarot card reading, they are going to instantly assume you've put in the time to learn this mysterious craft and know what you are talking about. Another benefit is that people tend to lose their inhibitions and openly ask for a tarot card or palm reading, when they see it done to others in a social setting.

Tarot cards and palmistry are skills that require a certain amount of practice, but the benefit in learning these skills is that the reader gives credit to the system, instead of themselves. In other words, anything in the reading that is inaccurate or unfavorable are simply attributed to "what the cards say."

Tricks of Guile - Mentalism

Mentalism is a field of magic that appears to be mind reading, when in fact it is simple magic and trickery. Doing a search online or in a book store will give a wealth of resources to incorporate a few mentalism tricks into your cold reading routine.

Here is one of the simplest mentalism mind reading tricks that always promises a good result, using tarot cards. The reader riffles quickly through the deck of cards and asks the subject to tell him when to stop. The subject then takes the card, not revealing it to the reader. The reader then gives a reading to the subject, describing their personality and concludes by saying, "Based on that reading, it is my guess that you would have pulled out the Ace of Cups. Am I right?" and, of course, that's what the reader is holding in their hand.

How the effect is done is incredibly simple. After shuffling the deck, the reader glances at the very bottom card and then cuts the deck. He will place his little "pinky" finger slightly over the edge of the bottom half of the cut. This keeps the cut separated, with the bottom card resting hidden on top of the little finger. He then riffles through the deck, telling the subject to say, "Stop" at any time. When the subject says 'stop,' the reader quickly moves the upper half of the deck forward and lifts it off, revealing the card at the bottom of the cut that he glanced at before the cut. (In magic, this is referred to as a "card force," and there are hundreds of ways of doing them.)

When the reading is over and the reader "guesses" at what card the subject "randomly" picked, it will tend to verify that the reader is the "real deal" and thus make every other aspect of the reading true and acceptable.

Appealing to the Seven Hidden Addictions

In the section of this book, you'll read in more detail about the Seven Hidden Addictions. A psychic can never fail by appealing to these powerful human needs. This is especially true of the addictions of "providing hope" and "the scapegoat."

When it comes to "providing hope," you will never lose out by providing someone with hope during a psychic reading. You can give them cautions, and let them know there are things they should pay attention to, but don't destroy their hope.

If there is a problem they are facing, you will do best to find a way to let them know it is not their fault - give them a scapegoat. I don't recommend you tell them they've been cursed or anything like that. Instead, reassure them that they've done all they could and that they are a good person.

It is also a good idea to let the person know that they are in some way needed and important to the people around them.

If you are going to go into doing psychic cold readings, make a point of reading and incorporating "The Seven Hidden Addictions" in your reading, and people will naturally love what you tell them.

Training for Unconscious Response

To my knowledge, this is the first time this trick has been revealed in writing, but it has been alluded to by magicians, who practice mind reading and mentalism tricks. Many psychic cold readers use it unconsciously, with great effect. It is called the "eye brow raise," using the raised eyebrow and head nod to get unconscious confirmation.

The reader starts by asking a question that they know or strongly suspect the subject will answer "yes." For example, noticing the watch on the right wrist, the reader will ask, in the tone of a statement, "You seem like someone who looks at things a bit differently than others. You are left-handed, aren't you?" But the reader will raise the eyebrows and nod, as if asking for confirmation. The subject will then respond. When they respond with a "yes," they will also unconsciously nod their head to the eyebrow raise. This act begins to train them to respond with unconscious signals. When the answer to a statement asked in this manner is "no," they will pause, which allows the reader to back track.

Here is an example of "mind reading" done in this way:

Reader: *I'd like to ask you to think of a memory; make sure it is a pleasant memory that you remember from way back.*

This directs the subject to go "way back" and find a pleasant memory. Already, the memories are being limited by the reader. The reader will then direct the questions, based on the subject's unconscious responses to the eyebrow raise, with nod.

This was when you were young... (eyebrow raise), *quite young...* (eyebrow raise, noting pause response)... *not too young... a teenager...* (subject gives an unconscious 'yes' nod)... *Okay, so you are a teenager... this is a special occasion...* (eyebrow raise and nod, not noticing a response)... *It is not that special... it is a regular day, but something nice is happening.... You are with friends... family members...* (Notice which they respond to - "friends" or "family members.")

Mediumship and Group Reading

This is the art of working with people who want to speak with a dead friend or relative. This does take some practice and experience to do well, but it is surprising how simple it can be.

Many people will do a psychic reading for a group of people. The reader would start by reading "someone in the group," without being specific who it is. This makes it even easier, because it is much easier to find someone who will agree that the reading applies to them. One such reading can be as follows:

"There is someone here who has lost someone... a close friend or family member. The loss happened during a celebration or holiday... that's how you remember it." During this open reading, the reader would be looking around for signs of unconscious agreement. Then look at the person who is responding to what they say.

Many cold readings do not involve fishing, vagueness or wild guessing. The key to a successful cold reading is the willingness, ability and effort of the client to find meaning and significance in the words of the psychic, astrologer, palm reader, medium or the like.

A medium claiming to get messages from the dead might throw out a string of ambiguous images to the client. "Father figure, the month of May, the Big-H, and H with an N sound, Henna, Henry, M, maybe Michael, teaching, books, maybe something published."

This list could mean different things to different people. To some people, it probably has no meaning. The client will either connect these dots or she won't. Clients of mediums who claim to get messages from the dead are very highly motivated clients. Not only do they have an implicit desire for immortality, they have an explicit desire to contact a dear loved one who has died. The odds are in favor of the medium that the client will find meaning in many different sets of ambiguous words and phrases. If she connects just a couple of them, she may be satisfied that the medium has made a connection to a dead relative. If she doesn't find any meaning or significance in the string, the medium still wins. He can try another string. He can insist that there is meaning here ,but the client just isn't trying hard enough to figure it out. He can suggest that some uninvited spirit guests are confusing the issue. It is a win-win situation for the medium, because the burden is not on him but on the client to find the meaning and significance of the words.

If you ever get a chance to see one of those psychic readers, who tell people about their dead friends and relatives, you will learn a lot about cold reading and watching for unconscious responses.

Dumb Blonde Mind Control

Dumb Blonde Mind Control refers to a specific strategy used mostly by women to control men. The strategy works best when it is a kind of a push-pull. That is to say, the promise (or hint) of easy sexuality (the pull), combined with a calculated helplessness and vulnerability (the push). It is the second half, the perception of vulnerability, that encourages the victims to make allowances, when they'd otherwise get angry (or catch onto the scam).

This push-pull is referred to in hypnosis as *fractionation*, where each time a person returns to a previous mental or emotional state, the intensity of the state or emotion grows.

The best 'dumb blondes' are often really approachable and personable - at first.

The ones who really know the game alternate between sexy and vulnerable; affection and rejection, in a sort of three-step process.

At first, the affection/rejection swing seems to be a reaction to something her subject is doing, and he begins to modify his behavior, thinking he's in control and stimulating her good behavior and moods. Actually, it is him that's responding to conditioning, a la Pavlov, and this is the first stage of compliance.

Then, when she's got pretty reliable compliance, her moods and reactions may become more overt rewards and punishments. She should always frame them as reactions, and emphasize her own vulnerability, to keep his defenses down. (How many times have you seen a guy doing something nice for his girlfriend, as a result of her being a bitch, and he not even quite knowing why he's doing it? I have several friends who, when asked why they are doing this, just shrug and reply, "Oh, well, it is just one of her little moods.")

Finally, she should alternate between sexy and vulnerable; affection and rejection, incongruously. He should be at a total loss as to why she reacts the way she does - sometimes. To achieve real control over her subject, she has to get him to believe he has her almost figured out. Almost. Thinking that he's almost got her will keep him hooked. Breaking the pattern will send him back to square one.

This is just one context in which this strategy can be used. It can be applied in other areas, too.

Consider a setting where a potential business partner promises investment capital for a project but acts ignorant about certain aspects of the project. So the subject gives a concession, in the form of more information. This is followed by a return to the promise of investment capital, then another requested concession. Ultimately, the controller-investor has all the concessions they need and completely withdraw their investment capital.

The only way to counter this strategy is to be aware of it, and make a note whether each concession has actually yielded any real measurable progress. If the "progress" is only a promise or a possibility and not something tangible, then all concessions must stop, until something measurable is returned.

Appealing to Basic Human Responses

In 2004, TV producer and author Blair Warren wrote and published the book, *The Forbidden Keys to Persuasion,* in which he describes what he calls "The 7 Hidden Addictions."

These "addictions" are responses that people have, almost as a reflex, and are often expressed as needs. They are called *addictions,* because we automatically respond to them, as if they were a drug.

These are the seven addictions:

Addiction #1: The need to be needed. This addiction goes to the heart of our need to know that we are special. When we are needed, our value is recognized. The process of expressing that need is simple and straight-forward, and Warren describes the process in six steps:

Step 1. Explain the situation as a whole. What is at stake? What is a dilemma?

Step 2. Explain the specific role the person can play in the situation.

Step 3. Emphasize the importance of the role.

Step 4. Point out how the person is uniquely qualified for the role.

Step 5. Openly acknowledge that your request will require a sacrifice on their part.

Step 6. Ask if you can count on them to help.

As you can see, this is a very simple tactic to implement, and it can be done in person and with any form of media.

Exercise:

Go through this process with someone. Anyone. It could be a family member, employee, friend or co-worker. Compare your results to any other way you try to motivate them.

Addiction #2: The need for a sense of hope, when an impasse occurs. People will automatically respond when given some form of hope in a tough situation.

Psychics hot lines make a damn fine living fulfilling this need. They tell people what they want to hear, and people are willing to pay for it.

Consider how many "self help" and "how to" books line the bookshelves.

This can easily be taken advantage of anytime a problem is recognized. If this is a process that will be repeated with the same subjects, it is best to have a good track record of rescuing from the impasse.

Exercise:

Anytime you ask something of someone, implement this process of letting them know they are needed.

Addiction #3: The need for a scapegoat. As much as people preach about taking responsibility for our lives, there is nothing more reassuring than knowing that the source of our troubles can be placed on someone else's shoulders.

Why? Because we want to believe our perception of reality is right (another hidden addiction). If our perceptions are correct, then we would not have problems, and any problems we perceive are not because of us. Providing a scapegoat prevents us from having to reevaluate that, in truth, our reality might be wrong.

A good example of this is in many weight loss commercials that say. "Have you tried to lose weight and feel frustrated, no matter what you do? It may be your metabolism." Giving the person a scapegoat - their metabolism - provides a *huge* amount of relief and an opportunity to provide relief, using the previous hidden addiction.

Consider how having an enemy motivates people to war. When a rival is identified, people will focus all their attention to the battle. Many governments, politicians and religious leaders have created an enemy, to help unify the group.

When speaking about this particular addiction, I always make a point of arguing in favor of taking responsibility for everything in our lives, good and bad. At the same time, it would be wise to never underestimate people's tendency to find fault anywhere but with themselves.

Exercise:

Test this out in anyway possible, just to see how people respond to it. Especially do it with those people who encourage taking complete responsibility for their lives. Even they will respond favorably.

Addiction #4: The need to be noticed and feel understood. One of the reasons cults can be so attractive to people is that they give, at least for a time, feelings of acknowledgment and acceptance.

One way that anyone can fulfill this need is to not just listen to what people say, but to take part in "active listening." Active listening is a simple process of repeating back what people tell you, without adding your own comments and interpretations.

There are several benefits to active listening for both parties. For the subject, it fulfills the need to be noticed and understood. Active listening provides a way that the subject can express their views, without judgment.

For the controller, active listening is a great substitute for going on the defensive, when being told something uncomfortable. All the controller needs to do is say, "So what you are saying to me is...." then rephrase what the subject has just said - and then remain silent. In many cases, the subject will take this for agreement, and the discussion will end.

Active listening also provides the controller with excellent information about the subject's perceptions and world views, because it allows for the subject to respond to what the controller has said. This can be very useful in elicitations of states and emotions.

Exercise:

Make a point of seeing how people respond to you, when you let them know you understand what they are expressing. Don't just say, "I agree" or "I understand." Demonstrate your new-found sense of understanding by actively communicating with them. Put aside any moral evaluations to what they are saying, and avoid getting defensive, if this is a personal issue involving you.

Addiction #5: The need to know things they don't or shouldn't know. You want to know a secret? So does everyone else. Being let in on a secret confirms that we are special, when it is provided by an outside source. When the secret is discovered independently, it tends to create a sense of power that "I know something you don't know."

Using this addiction is very easy. You can do it by referring to something that the subject can't know about yet, perhaps due to lack of training

A good salesman will never give away all the information about his product. If he's smart, he'll hold back and then "let you in on a secret."

There are two forces within someone when they are given a secret. Both are powerful. One is the force to tell the secret to others and receive an immediate reward for the knowledge. The other force is the one that comes from keeping the secret. This force is more lasting, yet less immediate, and grows more powerful, the longer you keep the secret. By keeping that secret, it builds a sense of strength that only the individual knows about.

When every effort is made to keep the secret then, if you are to reveal it, it becomes like a holy weapon that is only to be used in the most extreme situation, for the most devastating results.

Addiction #6: The need to be right. Our need to be right is based on our trust of our perceptions, because we rely on our senses for our lives. Being told we are wrong forces us to re-evaluate the trust we have in our senses. Often the issue of being wrong becomes more important than the issue being argued.

By letting someone know that they are right, you gain their rapport and establish that you are on their side.

But what if they are not right? Then you refer to the scapegoat, and let them know that they are wrong, but it is not their fault!

Let's suppose you are being challenged by someone. You want to maintain your position, but you want to make sure the other person is not told that they are wrong.

Another way to accomplish this is to acknowledge their point, while setting aside the issue. Phrases like, "Your point is well taken" and "I can appreciate where you are coming from" and "I'm glad you brought that up" make you appear to agree with them, without agreeing.

Exercise:

Note how many times during the next week you are involved in an exchange where someone is trying to be right. If your tendency is to argue for your point, try acting like a diplomat, and use one of the mentioned tactics, so that they will not feel challenged.

Addiction #7: The need to feel a sense of power. The key word for this addiction is "sense of power." As long as they feel they are in control, the opposite reality does not have to be shared with them. This is often done by pointing out that any action they take is a choice and entirely up to them.

Imagine a young person, named Chris, who is torn between a cult and his parents. His parents tell him that the group he is participating in is a cult, and they forbid him from going any further. At the same time, the cult will tell him, "No doubt, your parents love you. No one can blame them ,because they want what they think is best. Chris, you've lived long enough to know what's best for yourself. We trust your decision. We would certainly love your participation here, but you are an adult now, and that choice is ultimately up to you."

The cult has done something that Chris' parents did not. They treated him like an adult and gave the power of the decision up to him. By comparison, it is almost irresistible.

Exercise:

Take note of your interactions with people, and find out where in the exchange you can build the other person's sense of power and control. This does not have to compromise anything you are doing. You don't have to give up power to point out the power that someone else has. The easiest way to do this is to point out that they ultimately have the final choice in any deal.

Exercise:

This isn't hard. Consider the seven hidden addictions and how they are applied in everyday life. Take note when you recognize any of the hidden addictions being used, and use them liberally, yourself, and notice people's reactions.

Interviews & Interrogation

Mind Control has many outcomes. For the sake of getting the truthful answers to serious questions, it is ideal, and it has been polished to a razor-sharp edge. This process has been described in much more depth in the book by David Leiberman entitled, *Never Be Lied To Again*.

Getting the truth can be divided into a series of steps. If the truth is not given in the first step, the controller progresses to the next step.

Phase One – Three Attack-Sequence Steps

Step 1:

The objective here is to ask a question that does not accuse the person of anything but alludes to the person's possible behavior. The key is to phrase a question that sounds perfectly innocent to an innocent person, but like an accusation to the guilty.

Suspicion: You feel that your girlfriend was unfaithful the night before.

Question: Anything interesting happen last night?

Suspicion: You think a coworker told your secretary that you have a crush on her.

Question: Heard any good gossip recently?

Any answers, such as, "Why do you ask?" or "Where did you

hear that?" indicate concern on the person's part. He should not be seeking information from you, if he does not think that your question is leading. He should also not be interested in why you're asking the question, unless he thinks that you may know what he doesn't want you to know.

Step 2:

The objective here is to introduce a scenario, similar to what you suspect is going on, using specifics.

Suspicion: You suspect one of your salespeople has lied to a customer, in order to make the sale.

Question: Jim, I'm wondering if you could help me with something. It's come to my attention that someone in the sales department has been misrepresenting our products to customers. How do you think we can clear this up?

Suspicion: A hospital administrator suspects that a doctor was drinking while on duty.

Question: Dr. Marcus, I'd like to get your advice on something. A colleague of mine at another hospital has a problem with one of her doctors. She feels he may be drinking while on call. Do you have any suggestions on how she can approach the doctor about this problem?

If he's innocent of the charges, he's likely to offer his advice and be pleased that you sought out his opinion. If he's guilty, he'll seem uncomfortable and will assure you that he never does anything like that. Either way, this opens the door to probe further.

Step 3:

The objective here is to introduce a scenario, similar to what you suspect is going on, using general terms.

Suspicion: You think a student has cheated on his exam.

Question: Isn't it amazing how someone can cheat on a test and not realize that I was standing behind him the entire time?

Suspicion: You suspect a coworker of bad-mouthing you to your boss.

Question: It's amazing all the backstabbing that goes on around here, isn't it? And these people doing it think that it won't get back to the person involved.

Suspicion: You think that your girlfriend may be two-timing you.

Question: It's amazing how someone can be unfaithful and expect not to get caught.

A change in subject is highly indicative of guilt. However, if he finds your question interesting, and he's innocent, he might begin a conversation about it, since he's unafraid to discuss the subject.

Phase Two: Eleven Attack Sequences

Attack Sequence 1 - Direct Questioning

Stage 1: Ask your question directly.

* Give no advance warning of the subject you're about to bring up or of any feelings of mistrust.

* Never reveal what you know first. Ask questions to gather information, to see if it's consistent with what you already know.

* The way you present yourself can greatly influence the attitude of the other person. Three powerful tips for establishing and building rapport:

1. Matching posture and movements – if he has one hand in his pocket, you put your hand in yours.

2. Matching speech – if he's speaking in a slow, relaxed tone, you do the same.

3. Matching key words – if he's prone to using certain words or phrases, use them when speaking.

* Ask a question that you know will produce a response similar to how you expect him to react. In other words, if he waves his arms around, no matter what he's talking about, you want to know this.

* Use a relaxed and non-threatening posture, and square off, so that you're facing each other.

* Never, ever interrupt. You can't learn anything new, while you're talking. Ask open-ended questions.

Stage 2: Silence. The pressure of silence is incredible, especially for the person who is withholding information.

Stage 3: Really? At the end of his answer, respond with, "Really?"

Stage 4: Sudden Death. Follow with, "Is there anything you want to get off your chest?"

Attack Sequence 2 - Lead and Confine

Stage 1: Ask a leading question. For example, "You were back by two a.m. last night, weren't you?"

Stage 2: Reverse course. You've got to be kidding! For example, "I was hoping you did, so you would have gotten it out of your system. Please tell me that you've done it, so I know that it's over with."

Stage 3: This is not going to work. For example, "I thought you were somebody who had a sense of adventure. Someone who knows how to live a little."

Attack Sequence 3 - Time Line Distortion

Scenario: You suspect several employees in your store of stealing money.

Stage1: Setting the scene. Let the conversation turn casually to stealing and say, "Oh, I knew right from the start what was going on."

Stage 2: It's no big deal. "You had to know I knew. How else do you think you could have gotten away with it for so long? I hope you don't think I'm a complete idiot."

Stage 3: I appreciate what you've done. "I know that you were just going along with it, because you were scared of what the others would do. It's really okay. I know you're not that kind of person."

Attack Sequence 4 - Direct Assumption / Shot in the Dark

Stage 1: Set the scene. Be somewhat curt and standoffish, as if something heavy-duty is bothering you. This will cause his mind to race, to find ways to explain the "error of his ways."

Stage 2: I'm hurt. Say, "I've just found something out, and I'm really hurt (or shocked/surprised). I know you're going to lie to me, and try to deny it, but I just wanted you to know that I know." You establish that (a) he's guilty of something and (b) you know what it is.

Stage 3: Holding your ground. Say, "I think we both know what I'm talking about. We need to clear the air, and we can start by your talking."

Stage 4: Continue to hold your ground. Repeat phrases, such as, "I'm sure it will come to you" and "The longer I wait, the madder I'm getting."

Stage 5: Apply social pressure. "We were all talking about it. Everybody knows." Now he begins to get curious about who knows and how they found out. As soon as he tries to find out, you'll know he's guilty.

Attack Sequence 5 - The Missing Link

Scenario: You think that your mother-in-law may have hired a private investigator to follow you around.

Stage 1: List facts. Tell her something that you know to be true. "I know you're not very fond of me and that you objected to the wedding, but this time you've gone too far."

Stage 2: State your assumption. "I know all about the investigator. Why did you think that was necessary?"

Stage 3: The magic phrase. "You know what, I'm too upset to talk about this now." The guilty person will honor your request, because she won't want to anger you further. An innocent person will be mad at you for accusing her of something that she hasn't done and will want to discuss it now.

Attack Sequence 6 - Who, Me?

Stage1: Setting the scene. He suspects that his ex-girlfriend broke into his house. He phoned to let her know, in a very non-accusatory way, that there had been a break-in, and some items were missing. The following type of conversation would ensue:

Winston: The police are going to want to talk to everyone who had access to the house. Since you still have a key, they're going to want to speak with you. Just routine stuff, I'm sure. Of course, you're not a suspect.

Ex-Girlfriend: But I don't know anything about it.

Winston: Oh, I know. Just policy, I guess. Anyway, one of my neighbors said that she got a partial license-plate number on a car that was by my house that day.

Ex-Girlfriend: (After a long pause) Well, I was driving around your neighborhood that day. I stopped by to see if you were home. But when you weren't, I just left.

Winston: Oh, really? Well, they did a fingerprint test, too. That should show something.

Ex-Girlfriend: What test?

Winston: Oh, they dusted for prints and...

Stage 2: Inform non-accusatorily. Casually inform your suspect of the situation.

Stage 3: Introduce evidence to be rebutted. As you introduce the evidence, look to see if each of your statements is met by explanations from him as to how the evidence could be misunderstood.

For example, you suspect that a co-worker had shredded some of your files. You would first set the stage, by letting him know that you can't find some important files. Then say, "Well, it's a good thing my new secretary noticed someone by the shredder the other day. She said she recognized his face but didn't know his name." An innocent person would not feel the need to explain, in order to avert the possibility that he might be wrongly accused.

Stage 4: Continue. Continue with more facts that the person can try to explain away. But in actuality, as soon he starts to talk about why the situation might "look that way," you know you have him.

Attack Sequence 7 - Outrageous Accusations

Stage 1: Accuse him of everything. In a very fed-up manner, accuse him of doing every imaginable dishonest and disloyal act.

Stage 2: Introduce the suspicion. Now introduce the one thing you feel he really has done, and in an attempt to clear himself of the other charges, he will offer an explanation for his one slip-up.

Say, "I mean, it's not like you just stole a file, that would be fine. But all these other things are unspeakable." He responds, "No, I just stole that one file, because of the pressure to get the job done, but I would never sell trade secrets!"

The only way to prove his innocence to all of your outrageous accusations is to explain why he did what you really suspect of him of doing.

Stage 3: Step in closer. This increases anxiety in the guilty. He feels he's being closed in on.

Attack Sequence 8 - Is There a Reason?

Stage 1: Introduce a fact. For example, if you want to know if your secretary went out last night, when she said she was sick, you could say, "I drove by your house on the way home. Is there a reason your car wasn't in the driveway?" Had she been home sick, she would simply tell you that you were wrong – the car was in the driveway.

Stage 2: One more shot. "Oh, that's odd, I called your house, and I got your machine." If she's guilty, she will look for any way to make her story fit your facts.

Stage 3: Stare. Staring makes someone who is on the defensive feel closed in; your glare is infringing on her personal space, inducing a mental claustrophobia. Lock eyes with her and ask again.

Attack Sequence 9 - Third-Party Confirmation

Scenario: You suspect one of your employees is having someone else punch out on the time clock for him.

Stage 1: Accuse outright. After gaining the assistance of a friend or coworker, you have this person make the accusation for you. Such as, "Mel, I was talking to Cindy, and she told me she's getting pretty tired of your having someone else punch out for you, so you can leave work early." At this point, Mel is concerned only with Cindy's disapproval of his actions. Your friend is thoroughly believable, because we rarely think to question this type of third-party setup.

Stage 2: Are you kidding? "Are you kidding? It's common knowledge, but I think I know how you can smooth things over with her." See if he takes the bait. A person who's innocent would not be interested in smoothing things over with someone else, for something that he hasn't done.

Stage 3: Last call. "Okay. But are you sure?" At this point, any hesitation is likely to be a sign of guilt, because he's quickly trying to weigh his options.

Attack Sequence 10 - The Chain Reaction

Scenario: You suspect several employees in your store of stealing money

Stage 1: Setting the scene. In a one-on-one meeting with the employees, let them know that you're looking for someone to be in charge of a new internal theft program for the entire company.

Stage 2: The irony is… "We're looking for someone who knows how it's done. Now don't worry, you're not going to get in trouble. As a matter of fact we've known about it for some time. We were more interested in seeing how efficient you were. Quite impressive. Anyway, we feel that since you know how it's done, you'll know how to prevent it. Granted, it's pretty unusual, but this is an unusual instance."

Stage 3: I told them so. "You know, I told them that you would be too afraid to have an open discussion about this. They were wrong, I was right." Look for hesitation on his part. If he's guilty, he will be weighing his options. This takes time. An innocent person has nothing to think about. Only the guilty have the option of confessing or not.

Attack Sequence 11 - Condemn or Concern

Stage 1: I'm just letting you know. The key with this sequence is not to accuse, just to inform.

Let's say that you're working in the customer service department of a computer store. A customer brings back a non-working printer for an exchange, claiming that he bought it just a few days before. He has the all-important receipt and the printer is packed neatly in the original box. Upon inspecting the contents, you find that a necessary, expensive and easily removable component of the machine is missing; a clear indication of why the machine was not functioning properly. Here are two possible responses you might get, after informing the customer of your discovery.

Response 1. "I didn't take it out. That's how it was when I bought it." (Defensive)

Response 2. "What? You sold me a printer that has a missing part? I wasted two hours trying to get that thing to work." (Offensive)

The person who utters Response 2 has every right to be annoyed; it never crosses his mind that he's being accused of anything.

The person who gives Response 1 knows he never even tried to get the printer to work, because he took the part out. It doesn't occur to him to become angry. He assumes that he's being accused of removing the part and becomes defensive, when you inform him the part is missing.

Phase Three – Eleven Silver Bullets:
How to Get the Truth Without Beating It Out of Them

To convey honesty and truthfulness in your message, use the following techniques:

* Look the person directly in the eyes.
* Use hand movements to emphasize your message.
* Use animated gestures that are fluid and consistent with the conversation.

* Stand or sit upright – no slouching.
* Don't start off with any statements, such as, "To tell you the truth…" or "To be perfectly honest with you…"
* Face the person straight on. Don't back away.

Liars need an incentive to confess. The payoff for confessing needs to be immediate, clear, specific and compelling. You can't just tell a person what he'll gain by being truthful, or lose by continuing to lie.

You must make it real for him – so real, in fact, that he can feel, taste, touch, see and hear it. Make it his reality. Let him experience fully the pleasure of being honest and the pain of continuing the lie. Involve as many of the senses as you can, particularly visual, auditory and kinesthetic. Create images for the person to see; sounds for him to hear; and sensations that he can almost feel. You want to make this experience as real as possible. First, state the positives, then state the negatives, and then present the choice.

Silver Bullet 1: If You Think That's Bad - Wait Until You Hear This!

This bullet works well, because it forces the liar into thinking emotionally, instead of logically. It alleviates his guilt, by making him feel that he's not alone, and it throws him off, by creating a little anger and/or curiosity. Plus, he thinks that you and he are exchanging information, instead of his giving you something for nothing.

Sample question formation: "The reason I'm asking you these questions is that I've done some things that I'm not too proud of, either. I can understand why you might have… In a way, I'm almost relieved. Now I don't feel too bad." At this point, he will ask you to get more specific about your actions. But insist that he tell you, first. Hold out, and he'll come clean.

Silver Bullet 2: It Was an Accident. Really!

This is a great strategy, because it makes him feel that it would be a good thing to have you know exactly what happened. He did something wrong, true, but that is no longer your concern. You shift the focus of your concern to his intentions, not his actions. This makes it easy for him to confess to his behavior, and "make it okay," with the explanation that it was unintentional. He feels that you care about his motivation. In other words, you let him know that the source of your concern is not what he's done, but why he's done it.

Sample question formation: "I can understand that maybe you didn't plan on this happening. Things just got out of control, and you acted without thinking. I'm fine with that – an accident, right? But if you did this on purpose, I don't think that I could ever forgive you. You need to tell me that you didn't do it intentionally. Please."

Silver Bullet 3: The Boomerang

This bullet really throws a psychological curve ball. With this example, you tell him that he did something good, not bad. He's completely thrown off by this. For example, you want to see if your interviewee has lied on her resume.

Sample question formation: "As we both know, everybody pads his resume, just a bit. Personally, I think it shows guts. It tells me that the person isn't afraid to take on new responsibilities. Which parts were you most creative with on this resume?"

Silver Bullet 4: Truth or Consequences

With this bullet, you force your antagonist to work with you, or you both end up with nothing. This is the exact opposite of the "boomerang." Here, the person has nothing, unless he cooperates with you. Since you have nothing, anyway, (the truth), it's a good trade-off for you. Let's say you suspect that your housekeeper has stolen from you.

Sample question formation: "I'd rather hear it from you, first. I can live with what you did/what happened, but not with your lying to me about it. If you don't tell me, then it's over. If you tell me the truth, things can go back to how they were. But if you don't, then we have no chance here, and you'll have nothing."

Silver Bullet 5: Speak Now or Forever Hold Your Peace

Human beings place a premium on that which is scarce. Simply put, rare equals good. You can dramatically increase your leverage, by conveying that this is the only time that you will discuss this. Let him know that (a) this is the last chance he'll have to explain himself, and (b) you can get what you need from someone else.

Try increasing the rate of your speech, as well. The faster you speak, the less time he has to process the information, and it conveys as stronger sense of urgency. Give a deadline, with a penalty for not meeting it. Deadlines force action. If the guilty party thinks that he can always come clean, then he will take a wait-and-see approach, before tipping his hand. Let the person know that you already know and have proof of his action; and admitting his sins now will give him the opportunity to explain his side.

Sample question formations: "I want to hear it from you, now. After tomorrow, anything you say won't make a difference to me. I know what happened/what you did. I was hoping I would hear it from you, first. It would mean a lot to me to hear your side of it. I know there are two sides to every story, and before I decide what to do, I want to hear yours." Hearing this gives him the feeling he still has a chance, if he confesses. After all, what really happened can't be as bad as what you heard. Confessing now is a way of cutting his losses.

Silver Bullet 6: Reverse Course

You convey to him that what happened or what he did was a good thing, insofar as it allows you and he to establish an even better relationship - personal or professional. You give him an opportunity to explain why he took that choice. You also blame yourself.

Sample question formation: "I understand why you would have done that. Clearly, you wouldn't have, unless you had a good reason. You were probably treated unfairly or something was lacking. What can I do to help, so that it doesn't happen again?" Keep interjecting the following phrases: "I take full responsibility for your actions. Let's work together to see how we can avoid this from happening again. I understand completely. You were right to do what you did."

Silver Bullet 7: I Hate To Do This, But You Leave Me No Choice

This is the only strategy that involves threat. You let him become aware that there are going to be greater ramifications and repercussions than just lying to you – things that he never thought about. You rely on his imagination to set the terms of the damage that you can inflict. His mind will race through every possible scenario, as his own fears turn against him.

Sample question formation I: "I didn't want to have to do this, but you leave me no choice." This will propel him to respond, "Do what?" At this point, he's waiting to see what the trade-off will be. But do not commit yourself to an action. Let him create in his own mind scenarios of what you will do, unless he confesses.

Sample question formation II: "You know what I can do, and I'll do it. If you don't want to tell me now, don't. I'll just do what I have to do." After this statement, pay close attention to his response. If he focuses on what you will do to him, the odds lean more toward guilty. However, if he reasserts that he's done nothing, he may, in fact, be innocent of your accusation. The guilty person needs to know the penalty, in order to determine if it makes sense for him to stick to his story.

Silver Bullet 8: I Guess You're Not Allowed

Never underestimate the power of appealing to a person's ego. Sometimes you want to inflate it, and others times you want to attack it. This bullet is for attacking. It's truly saddening how fragile some people's egos are.

Sample question formations: "I think I know what it is – you're not allowed to tell me. Somebody else is pulling the strings, and you'll get in trouble. You'd tell me the truth, if you could, but you don't have the power to do so."

Silver Bullet 9: Higher Authority

As long as the person believes that you are on his side, he'll take the bait. All you have to do is let him know that anything he's lied about can now be cleared up in seconds. However, if anyone else finds out about it later, it's too late. Let's say that you want to know if your secretary leaves early, when you're out of the office.

Sample question formation: "The vice president from corporate is coming in today. He's asked about your hours, so I'm going to tell him that you come in early on the days that you leave early. Do you remember what days last month you finished up early and took off?" This is disarming, and you're not yelling at her or demanding answers. You're on her side, and you're going to work together to smooth things over.

Silver Bullet 10: The Great Unknown

You can obtain maximum leverage, by explaining how the ramifications of his deceit will be something that the suspect has never known before. Even if he believes that you are limited in what you can do to him and in what the penalty will be, the severity of the penalty can be manipulated in two major ways, to make it appear much more severe - *time* and *impact*.

* Time: Give no indication of when the penalty will occur. When things happen unexpectedly, the degree of anguish is more potent.

* Impact: Convey that his entire life will be disrupted and drastically altered for the worse. He needs to see that this event is not isolated and will instead have a ripple effect. When bad things happen, we are often comforted in knowing that it will soon be over, and the rest of our life will remain intact and unaffected. But if these things are not assured, we become increasingly fearful and concerned.

Silver Bullet 11: I Couldn't Care Less

A primary law governing human nature is that we all have a need to feel significant. Nobody wants to be thought of as unimportant, or feel that his ideas and thinking are irrelevant. Take away a person's belief that he has value, and he'll do just about anything to reassert his sense of importance. Your apathy toward the situation will unnerve him immensely. He will begin to crave recognition and acceptance, in any form. He needs to know you care what happens, and if talking about his misdeeds is the only way he can find out, he will.

Sample question formations: "I know, and I just don't care. This is not for me. I've got other things to think about. Maybe we'll talk some other time. You do what you have to do, that's fine with me." To be more powerful, stare at him. When you stare at someone, he often feels less significant and will seek to reassert his value.

III. Tactics for Detecting Deceit and Gathering Information in Casual Conversations
General Conversations

1. Ask-a-Fact:

During the conversation, simply ask general, clear questions pertaining to your suspicion. This causes the person you are questioning to recall information. If he's lying, he'll take a while to answer, because he first has to check his response mentally to be sure it makes sense. Made-up stories do not have details, because they never happened!

Ask questions that will give you an objective, not a subjective response. For instance, if you think an employee was home, when he said he would be away on vacation, don't ask him how he enjoyed the weather in Florida, but rather ask, "Did you rent a car?" Once he answers "yes" to any question, ask for more detail. If he's lying, he'll try to keep the facts straight and will take his time answering further questions.

2. Add-a-False Fact:

Add a fact, and ask the person to comment on it. This fact is one that you've made up, but one that sounds perfectly reasonable. For example, if you wanted to know if someone really, indeed, went on a safari to Africa, you mention that your uncle, who works as a customs officer at the Nairobi airport told you that everyone going to Africa was given special instructions on how to avoid malaria. As soon as he validates your claim, in an attempt to back up his assertion that he has gone to Africa, you know that his story is untrue. Otherwise, he would simply say that he doesn't know what your uncle is talking about. Here are the criteria:

* Your statement has to be untrue
* It has to sound reasonable
* Your assertion has to be something that would directly affect the person, so he would have first-hand knowledge of this "fact."

3. Support-a-Fact

In this sequence, you take what the person says and request proof, but in a very non-threatening manner. For example, in the case of the person who claimed he had gone on a safari, you might let him know that you would love to see pictures of the trip. If he offers up a reason why you can't see the pictures, then this should arouse some suspicion.

4. Expand-a-Fact

Use this clue to determine how far someone is willing to go to get what she wants. All you do is expand on a fact that she has already offered. If she just goes on, without correcting you, then you know that she may be lying about what she's said so far and/or is willing to lie to get you to see her point. For example, your secretary asks you for the rest of the day off, because she's not feeling well. You might say, "Oh, of course, if you've got a fever and a bad headache, by all means, take off." She never claimed to have these symptoms. You merely expanded on her statement.

Mind Control 101

Special Occasions

1. Third-Party Protection

This tactic is used, if someone is reluctant to tell you something that involves another person. You have to appeal to his ego, and let him forget that he's telling tales out of school. The conversation needs to be positive. The other person must feel as if he's doing a good thing, by answering your question.

Scenario A: Your attorney is telling you about a case that a fellow attorney screwed up on. Simply asking, "What did he do wrong?" would probably get you nowhere. However, by turning it around, you create an incentive for him to tell you. Ask, "Had you handled the case, what would you have done differently?"

Scenario B: While chatting with Brad, one of your sales people, you would like to find out why Susan's sales figures are low. But simply asking him why she's not doing well might prove fruitless. Ask, "What areas do you think Susan can improve in?"

2. The Power Play

Sometimes the person reluctant to tell the truth is in a position of power. In these situations, it's usually inappropriate and futile to become argumentative. In these instances, you want to bring the conversation to a personal level.

Scenario: You're trying to sell to a buyer, who doesn't want to buy and is not giving you a reason that you truly believe. Your objective will be to get to the real objection. "I do this for a living. My family relies on me to support them. Clearly, we have a fine product, and you're a reasonable man. Would you mind telling me what I did to offend you?" Now your buyer is caught off guard and will undoubtedly follow with, "Oh, you didn't offend me. It's just that…"

3. Hurt Feelings

Someone is lying to you to protect your feeling – perhaps one of those little white lies. A touch of guilt makes the other person re-evaluate his approach.

Scenario: You feel that the truth is being withheld from you, for your own benefit. "I know you don't want to offend me, but you're hurting me more by not being perfectly honest. If you don't tell me, no one else will. If I can't count on you for this, I don't know what I would do."

4. It's a Matter of Opinion

The following is an excellent method for detecting deceit in a person's opinion.

Scenario: You're not sure if your boss really likes your idea for a new advertising campaign, even though she says she does.

"Do you like the concept for my new idea?"

"Sure. It's very original."

"Well, what would it take for you to *love* the idea?"

5. I Don't Know

This response can stall a conversation and leave you searching for answers. Sometimes it's just easier to say, "I don't know," which is often why we say it, in the first place. Either way, when you hear, "I don't know," try some of the following responses:

* Okay, then why don't you tell me how you've come to think the way you do?

* I know you don't know, but if you were to guess, what do you think it might be?

* What emotion best describes what you're thinking right now?

* What one word comes closest to describing what you're thinking?

In all these responses, you're taking the pressure off. You acknowledge the person's difficulty in answering. You then seem to be asking her to provide something else, when in reality, your new question is aimed at getting your initial question answered.

6. I'm Simply Embarrassed

The person may lie to you out of embarrassment. The usual tactics don't work here, because the person probably isn't obligated to tell you and more than likely will have nothing to gain by doing so. Therefore, you need to create an incentive for telling the truth, in an environment that makes him feel comfortable.

Scenario: You think the new intern mixed up two piles of papers and shredded the documents that were supposed to be copied.

"Nelson, if you're the one who did this, it's all right. I remember when I first started here. What I'm going to tell you is between you and me, okay? Good. I once made copies of a confidential memo, instead of the lunch menu, and placed a copy in each person's mailbox."

This instantly puts the other person at ease. It shows that you trust him, and he also feels obligated to share with you something he's done that he feels uncomfortable with.

7. Divide and Conquer

This is situation where there are two or more people from whom you can get the truth.

Scenario: Several of your sorority sisters pulled a practical joke, and you want to find out who is responsible.

"Jennifer, who did this is not important. I don't even care. What is important is our friendship. I want to know that I can trust you. I think I can, but I need for you to speak honestly with me. It's not that I'm so concerned with who did it – only that you are truthful with me about it."

If you don't get anywhere with her, go to someone else with the same speech.

8. Professional Reliance

When dealing with professionals:

* Always, if possible, get a second opinion. It's easy to do and can save you a lot of heartache.

* Make sure the person is licensed, insured and registered to do the actual work.

* Have your agreement drawn up in writing. Oral contracts aren't worth it.

* Ask for referrals or testimonials.

If he balks at any one of these points, you might want to take your business elsewhere. Finally, the following strategy should give you an accurate insight into the person's intentions. They key is to ask for the *opposite* of what you really want.

Scenario: Let's say that your travel agent suggests the Five-Day Cruise Getaway vacation package for you. You're looking to really let loose; you want a trip that will be non-stop fun, but you're not sure if she's pushing this package for the commission or if she really believes that it's a great deal.

"The brochure looks great, Sandy. I just want to make sure that this is not one of those party boats. I'm looking for some rest and relaxation. Is this that kind of trip?"

By asking your question this way, you will know the intentions of your travel agent and the answer to your question. If she answers yes, then you know that the cruise is not for you, or she is lying to get your business.

9. I Don't Know and I Don't Care

Few things are more frustrating than dealing with someone who just doesn't give a damn. Why? Because you don't have a whole lot to work with. You've got zero leverage. He's got nothing at risk, so you've got little bargaining power. You simply have to change the equation, so he's got something at stake.

Scenario: You take your car to the mechanic, and he tells you it will be fixed by Friday. But you just know that something is going to come up, and it will be sitting in his garage all weekend. "Okay, Joe. Tomorrow's fine. Just so you know, my wife is pregnant, and she's due any day. That's our only car, so if you can think of any reason why it may not be ready by Friday, you've got to let me know now."

10. I Just Heard

Most people who lie usually confide in at least one other person. It's important to let this person believe that you already know the truth, and then add your emotional reaction to it. For example, some general statements that would be said to the person whom you believe knows the truth:

* Sympathy: "I can't believe what Sam did. I am truly very sorry. If there's anything I can do for you or whatever, please just let me know, okay?

* Humor: "Mary, is Joe a magnet for odd things or what? He just told me, and I still can't believe it."

Directing the Conversation

You can steer a conversation in any direction that you choose. You can do this very efficiently with just a few well chosen words. After he makes a statement, you can use the following key words to direct the flow of information in any way that you choose. They can be used to extract information from any conversation.

* Meaning ... Saying this word after he speaks directs his thinking and the conversation toward the larger picture, giving you a better look at his overall position. He will offer the reason for the position.

* And ... This response gives you more lateral information. You'll be able to gather additional facts.

* So ... This response makes him get more specific, giving you the details of his position.

* Now ... This response makes him translate his position into a specific action. He will proceed to tell you exactly what he means and how it applies to you.

Getting Specific

Sometimes you'll get an answer, but it doesn't do you much good. Here are a couple ways of narrowing it down.

* In Response to an Opinion or Belief:

"I don't think the meeting went very well."

"Compared with what?" or "How poorly did it go?"

* In Response to a Reluctance to Commit:

"I don't know if I could."

"What, specifically, prevents you?" or "What would have to happen for you to be able to?" or "What would change if you did?"

Let the Truth be Told

These simple words work better than any others do:

"Because" - We're programmed to accept an explanation as valid, if it follows this word.

"Let's" - This word generates group atmosphere and initiates a bandwagon effect; it's positive and creates action.

"Try" - This little word is a powerful motivator, because it has a "what's the harm" mentality. For example, "Let's give it a try, because if it doesn't work, we can always go back to the way it was."

Clearly, you haven't introduced any reason for the person to take action, yet it seems to make sense, just the same.

Don't accuse someone by asking, "Why did you take five dollars from petty cash?" If you want to know if he took the money, simply say, "The money that we take from petty cash? Let's try to keep it to fewer than ten dollars at a time, because it works out better that way."

Taking Control

If in a situation where you are unable to speak, because the person keeps talking or interrupting, use some zingers like these. They play on two susceptible angles of human nature – ego and curiosity.

"You're a smart person; let me ask you a question."
"I know that you would want me to ask you this."
"You're the only person who would know the answer to this."
"I hope this news doesn't upset you."
"Along those lines…"

It's easy to change conversation, when you begin with the other's last thoughts.

IV. Mind Games
A Strong Defense: Avoiding The Lie

The best time to deal with a lie is before it turns into one. The following is a technique for cutting a suspicion off at the pass, before it turns into deception.

Method 1

This is the method you use when you want the truth, as it relates to a person's previous behavior. Here is a possible scenario. A parent suspects that her twelve-year-old son is smoking cigarettes.

Approach: "I know all about the smoking and the sneaking around. You know I'm not happy about that, but I just want you to promise me that you won't drink alcohol, until you're twenty-one."

This is by far the finest approach, because it works on so many levels. First, it takes a forward assumptive stance - the parent "knows all about the smoking." Second, it uses two truisms. The phrases "sneaking around" and "you know I'm not happy about that" set the tone for honesty.

The child hears two things that he knows to be true. He was sneaking around, and his mother is unhappy about his smoking. He is, therefore, willing to accept at face value what follows. Third, the mother gives her son an easy out. All he has to do is promise not to drink, and he's home free. There's no threat or punishment, just honest statements, followed by a deal that he believes to be true, as well.

The guidelines to keep in mind for this procedure are as follows:
* Assume your suspicion as fact

* State at least two truisms (facts that you both know to be true)
* Switch the focus from a threat to a request
* The request should be easy for him to accept, and sound reasonable

Method 2

This method is used when you want the truth, as it relates to a new decision. It is a simple but highly effective strategy to avoid being deceived. Oftentimes, someone wants to tell us the truth, but it's easier to tell a lie, instead. The person knows the answer you want to hear and will give it to you whether he believes it or not. However, if he doesn't know what you want, then he won't be able to deceive you. Read the following examples, and notice how well the second phrasing masks your true question.

* Would you like me to cook for you tonight?"
"Do you feel like eating in or out tonight?"
* I'm thinking of asking Rhonda out. What do you think of her?"
"What do you think of Rhonda?"

Know Thy Enemy: Knowing the Liar and His Intentions

The following example illustrates a process that is becoming very popular in employee screening tests. The questions below are asked the prospective employee, to determine if he is an honest person. If you really wanted the job, how would you answer these questions?

"Have you ever stolen anything in your life?"
"Have you ever run a red light?"
"Do you have a friend who has ever shoplifted?"

Many of us would have to answer "yes" to most of these questions. And that is precisely the answer a prospective employee is looking for. Why? Because the *honest* answer is "yes," for most of us.

The employer's task is finding those who are honest about it. Stealing a pack of gum when you were twelve years old doesn't make you a bad person or an undesirable employee.

Let's say that Martha's teenage son, who has been away from home and living on the streets for the past two years, wants to come home. Knowing that her son is addicted to cocaine, she is worried about whether he can actually clean up his act. She could tell him that he can move back in, only if he enrolls in a drug rehabilitation program. He will probably agree to this, whether he plans to do it or not. Instead, she tells her son that he can move back in, if he quits cold turkey - never doing another drug, whatsoever. Her son's answer will reveal his commitment to getting well, which is the real concern. Obviously, her son can hardly get rid of his addiction instantly. So if he indicates that he can, she knows that he's lying about his intention to get well. However, if he says that he can't but will make strides toward getting better, she will know that he is sincere in his pursuit of wellness.

Gaslighting Old & New

The origin of the word "gaslighting" refers to the 1944 movie "Gaslight," in which a husband attempts to make his wife appear insane, so he might commit her to a hospital. He does so by manipulating her environment ,with the objective to have her doubt her ability to interpret reality.

As a modern practice, gaslighting is any process designed to cause someone to doubt their judgment, perceptions or reality, so they may more easily accept another judgment, perception or reality that's offered to them.

Gaslighting happens every day, when someone attempts to have you reevaluate your conclusions, so that you will more readily accept their suggestions. In other words, it is a central feature of human communication and *this happens all the time.*

The typical form of gaslighting occurs by simply telling someone they are wrong. Of course, this has a limited effect, because it instantly creates resistance. Better to be subtle.

So, the more subtle ways of gaslighting:

Repetitive Questions & Slight of Mouth

Asking a series of even the most innocent questions about one's perceptions causes the individual to examine how these perceptions are constructed.

There is a method of selling called "Socratic Selling," in which questions are used by the sales person to gain information about the buyer's needs. (This is based upon the Socratic teaching method, where the teacher asks questions of the student to provoke critical thinking).

The questions asked are:
"How does this fit in the picture?"
"Would you elaborate on ?"
"What else should I know about ?"
"How does this affect you?"
"What makes this urgent?"
....and so on.

Each time these questions are asked, they focus the buyer on the need, instead of the cost or whatever might be the buyers objection to buying right away.

The pentacle of this form of gaslighting is called "Slight of Mouth." Slight of Mouth came about when NLP developer, Richard Bandler, was witnessed to never lose an argument.

When asked a series of slight of mouth questions, it forces the individual to reevaluate their belief, perception or reality, until they can no longer have the strength or stamina to hold it as real.

Slight of Mouth can take various forms. Here are a sample list of types of Slight of Mouth questions:

Questioning the Source:
"Where did you hear that from?"
"What could cause you to make that decision?"
"According to whom?"
"Have you checked the source?"
"How did you reach that conclusion?"
"Who told you to think that?"
"Well, it is possible that's based on faulty logic, isn't it?"

Questioning the Possibility:
"How is it possible to see it in that way, when you know you have better options?"

Questioning the Intent:
"What possible benefit could you lose out on by thinking that?"

Questioning the Methodology:
"How did you come to that conclusion?"

Questioning the Consequences:
"Have you considered exactly what thinking that is going to lead to?"

Giving a Counter-Example:
"Have you thought of all the cases where that wouldn't be the case, like (give an example)?"

Going to the Extreme:
"You know, if that were true, it would mean that (give an exaggerated and ridiculous outcome)."

Asking for a Different Perspective:
"You know if that were true, wouldn't everyone see it that way?"

Considering the Opposite Conclusion:
"How would (describe an opposing perception or belief) actually help you more easily get what you want?"

Questioning Who They Are:
"Are you really the type of person who wouldn't consider another possibility?"

If the controller creates a warm and friendly setting, like an instructional opportunity, and asks his subject a series of these questions, in a caring and supportive fashion, the results are amazing. The subject will completely reevaluate anything that they've been thinking.

The key is to do it in such a way that the subject is not threatened. This could begin as a series of written questions and followed by a get-to-know-you type of interview.

Consider that advertising does this all the time, in various ways.

Referring to the Unseen

Suffice to say that, anytime an expert talks about something that his listeners don't have a general knowledge about, he is using one of the most common methods of Mind Control.

When an expert in the field of psychiatry responds to his client's anger as a "complex," it forces the client to consider that there are things to be considered that are yet unknown.

Cults are notorious for pointing out things that are intended to be outside the normal person's awareness. This is usually done by creating a special language that is unique to the group. By doing that, it makes the uninitiated willing to put aside their assumptions to learn more.

This is also characteristic of specialized careers. All you have to do is listen to lawyers argue tax law, and you will realize that there are things you don't know about yet.

For you to use this form of gaslighting in an simple and easy way, all you have to do is remember the power of bullshit. Anytime you speak with authority about something, using unknown terms or using a common term in a new way, people will yield to your authority.

This can be done to encourage good behavior:

"...the more you attach your appreciation to the wholeness of the other person, the more you allow them to access the unconscious recognition of their own completeness."

And to discourage bad behavior:

"...by creating the acknowledgment of personal unconscious dysfunction within the in-the-moment awareness of responses and behaviors, one can initiate cessation of these dysfunctions, by the diligent application of awareness."

When spoken with authority, nonsense can be a powerful tool of Mind Control.

Refer to the Mystical

This has some similarity to "Refer to the Unknown" but is more about presenting yourself as simply knowing more than the other person. This can most easily be done by making mention of things that they have no knowledge of.

Think of when you go to any doctor, and you overhear them speaking in terms that sound like a doctor. As long as you don't know what they talking about, you are going to naturally assume that they do.

To use this in whatever field you want, just think of the terms or phrases that your subject has no idea about.

Reveal the Secret Thoughts of Others

Think what would happen if someone from your group of friends told you that most of the people within the group thought you were annoying and loud? Further, that no one wanted to tell you, and so they've been trying to act polite in your presence.

For most people, this would cause them to doubt themselves; a perfect example of gaslighting.

This is a common strategy among cults where a lead person in the group takes someone aside to reveal that others believe them to be unworthy of the next initiation. The result is that they work harder and are much more willing to do anything that might put them back into favor.

This is a fairly negative example, and it is very easy to use in this way, but it is equally powerful to use in a positive way.

An example of this form of positive gaslighting was written about by Blair Warren, in his book The *Forbidden Keys to Persuasion*. He describes how his young son got an A+ on a report card, and while tucking him into bed told him, "You know your mother couldn't stop bragging about you; she was so proud of you, but you can't let her know I told you."

This positive form of gaslighting bolstered his son's self-image and motivated him to keep his grades up.

The example is of the Prodigal Son, who leaves home and, when he returns, he expects to be seen as the black sheep of the family. Instead, he is told that he has always been loved and never thought ill of, even during his absence. He is accepted and explained that he did nothing wrong and welcomed back into the family.

Being able to orchestrate this for a subject creates an unexpected sense of acceptance, revealing the secret thought of acceptance to the subject.

Pointing Out Inconsistencies

Like "Revealing the Secret Thoughts of Others," Pointing out Inconsistencies is a gaslighting technique that can be used either to undermine a subject's confidence or to build it up.

Consider the early days of 'est.' The seminar participants were told the importance of keeping their commitments. They would start a diet and be off it in a week. They would commit to being a more caring spouse, only to return to their old habits. After having this hammered into them, hour after hour, they would completely give up on their own perceptions of themselves, creating complete doubt.

The constructive way to doing this is fairly simple. When your subject is in doubt, provide evidence of the contrary, based on their actions. As an example, someone who is feeling frustrated with their creative ability can be bolstered by simply pointing out all the times they were creative, either in writing, art or decision making.

Defining Reactions

"Defining Reactions" refers to an often used tool in psychotherapy, in which the therapist interprets and defines the client's response or reaction.

A typical example of this is when a client becomes angry or defensive, and the therapist defines the reaction as a "complex." Other self-improvement/personal growth trainings have their own terminology. They may refer to someone's response as an "addiction," and then define it as an *addiction* is something that you have to have happen, whether it benefits you or not.

Other terms include "issues," being "on it," to which you must "get off it," "a case," "an engram," just to name a few.

Defining reactions allows the subject to put aside their present interpretations of how they are reacting, and substitute the operator's meaning. In order for this to have any strong effect, a great deal of rapport and/or transference needs to be present.

Use Group Pressure

"None of us is dumber than all of us." ~ Anonymous

The power of group pressure can't be underestimated.

There is an often duplicated experiment, in which one person is put in a group under the pretense that they will evaluate pictures. In the beginning of the experiment, they all agree on common colors and dimensions of images. As the experiment continues, the group begins to agree on things that are obviously incorrect, leaving the unwitting subject to deal with the group pressure. In the majority of cases, the subject eventually agreed with the group; that green is blue, that the short line is, in fact, longer than the one they are comparing it to.

The subject will eventually doubt what they are seeing. The gaslighting is complete.

Another manifestation of this is obvious in mob actions. In the safety of a mob, people will tend to do things far outside their normal behavior. Just watch riots in action, and you can see this clearly. No one person will singularly throw a petrol bomb into a cop car on their own, but given group protection and encouragement, someone in a group of people will do it without hesitation.

Exercise:

Take a look at the examples in your daily life of gaslighting. Once you understand the concept, you can begin to recognize them everywhere.

Final Note

Gaslighting, aside from a tool of Mind Control, is also used as a tool of revenge. If this is your goal, the book I can recommend to you is *GASLIGHTING: How To Drive Your Enemies Crazy*, by Victor Santoro. The book is truly devious and has every step one can use to make your enemy think they are insane, and not get caught. Use it with caution.

Pharmacological Mind Control

Required Disclaimer:
Neither the author or publisher encourages the use of drugs. Drugs possess inherent dangers to the user and severe legal consequences for anyone caught giving drugs to another.

On a personal note, I found it very uncomfortable writing about certain aspects of using drugs for Mind Control.

Cigarettes

Seriously, one can't study Mind Control, without looking at the tobacco industry. For the first time, smoking tobacco is very seldom a pleasurable experience. Add to that the bad health effects and the contemporary social stigma of smoking, it is a wonder how millions of people take up the habit.

So how do you make a billion dollars a year selling a product that stinks and makes people sick? You use Mind Control!

As a drug, nicotine is only mildly addictive. This is largely dependent on the person. Some people become more addicted to it than others.

Combine that with advertising that tells the population that smoking will make you cool, manly, sexy or whatever and making it a product that is within the price range of even the most destitute, and you've got the hottest selling product in the world.

Another factor is that tobacco was promoted as a central agricultural economy for many, and that builds strong political support.

Mind Control 101

Alcohol

The oldest and most common Mind Control drug used is also the most available - alcohol. Alcohol tends to remove inhibitions. That's common knowledge, after a couple of thousand years of use. As a tool of Mind Control, the effects are short-lived and can be used only to get the most ephemeral outcomes.

Its only other use as a Mind Control drug is like that of many drugs, to maintain the user's addiction enough to keep them distracted from other issues. Alcohol has been proven to be quite effective at that. A nation that can maintain the fine balance that keeps its citizens productive and drunk can get away with quite a bit.

MDMA

MDMA, better known as ecstasy, has a tendency to create a deep sense of connection and love for the people who use it. When taken under the right circumstances, it magnifies any warmth and love and can create a deep sense of love. Taken in a group, it will bring together all the members of the group.

This intense feeling of connection can bring people to do and say things they normally wouldn't, sometimes bringing about embarrassment, when the drug's effect has worn off. Assuming the behavior is what the operator wants, it would be necessary to create a very supportive atmosphere that supports and encourages the new behaviors, when the drug is not used.

It has been published on the internet that when one combines MDMA with anti-anxiety drugs, like Valium or Adavan, compliance to do normally unacceptable behaviors is dramatically increased. It should also be noted that these two drugs alone may not be enough and that an atmosphere of trust and rapport continue to be equally important factors to achieving this high level of compliance.

LSD and Other Psychedelics

The effects of LSD (lysergic acid diethylamide) have been well documented as one of the most powerful psychoactive hallucinogens on the black market. It is the best known and most researched psychoactive drug. It is active at extremely low doses and is most commonly available on blotter or in liquid form.

Under the influence of LSD, people see images, hear sounds and feel sensations that seem real but do not exist. In addition, mood changes will occur throughout the period the drug is active, based on the user's mental state. It has been noted that the effects of LSD are equivalent to having a case of short-term schizophrenia, where nothing you are perceiving is, in fact, real.

Chronic effects of the drug can be positive and negative. Positive effects include spiritual contact and self-exploration; the most severe negative effect is known as LSD psychosis.

Because the effects seem so real, LSD has been billed as a drug that expands one's perceptions.

Many users are quite able to occasionally use LSD, without it effecting their everyday interactions. But it has been noted that frequent and prolonged use increases the probability that users will alter the normal reality testing abilities and have "flashbacks," which relive the drug state, even when the drug is not present in their system.

Its use for the purposes of Mind Control require slightly more preparation than the mere casual user.

In many shamanic cultures, where psychoactive drugs are used as part of an initiation, LSD has been used within a ritual setting, to create a tension of anticipation in the subject and, at the same time, create an atmosphere of safety. It has been rightly stated that the set and setting of rituals is central to creating a positive and powerful experience for the subject, when these types of drugs are involved. Do it at the wrong place or time, and the results will be very uncomfortable for the user. If the user begins the ritual in a stressed condition or bad mood, it may not be very pleasurable.

So, set and setting plus the rapport that the subject has with the other participants are important. Assuming that the controller has set up the environment appropriately, so that it is safe and comfortable, the controller can begin to introduce the beliefs, doctrines or behaviors they wish to teach and instill.

The most noted case of this being practiced is the infamous Charles Manson family of the 1960s. During this group's LSD trips, Manson would have the participants engage in sex orgies. If one participant found a sexual act unappealing, and resist participating, Manson would force them to perform every imaginable sexual act, and frame it as "overcoming your parents' issues."

Mind Control 101

The goal was to break down all the subjects' resistance and inhibitions, to do what they were told. The results were dramatic.

Using this method, along with other methods of cult indoctrination and Mind Control, Manson assigned several of his followers to perform the brutal murders of pregnant Hollywood actress Sharon Tate, along with Leno and Rosemary LaBianca, in a bizarre rampage that Manson thought would bring about a race war, in which he would rise up as the new messiah.

As a historical note, the U. S. military used LSD during military interrogations on unsuspecting prisoners, to increase anxiety. The terror and trauma were so profound that it created long term effects, even after they were released from prison.

Sodium Pentathol and Sodium Amitol

These are in a class of drugs known as "hypnotics," which depress the higher functions of the nervous system and cause a person to be more open to suggestions. These are also known as "truth serums," because they inhibit the faculties for deception.

According to the book *Deeper Insights into the Illuminati Formula,* by Fritz Springmeier & Cisco Wheeler, a huge secret government conspiracy exists to create Mind Control slaves.

The focus of the Mind Control programming is referred to as "trauma based Mind Control" and is very shocking, as it blatantly violates all moral and ethical rules of how to treat another human being. The subject was repeatedly put through cycles of programming and torture, so that they learned to follow orders to the letter, without question or judgment. Some of this alleged work includes the use of drugs.

Here is an excerpt from the book:

PROGRAMMING DRUGS

Acetophenzine aka Tindal - this anti-psychotic has been used on multiples; it mutes anxiety, suspiciousness and delusions; it would fall more into the control category of uses, rather than for actual programming.

Amines - this is a general term for many types of the brain's own chemicals used to produce moods, and feelings.

Damiana, aka **Mex. Witching Herb** - the extract is used with other herbs, during programming for a relaxed pleasure state. An example is Damiana-Biack, Kava Kava, Valerian, Skullcap, Wild Lettuce, Opium, which makes an "it's-nothing-but-a-dream" state.

Chloral hydrate - which is a hypnotic put in pill form, such as chioral betaine, Beta-Chlor and given with something like a glass of milk. About 500 mg. of Chloral hydrate are given for a hypnotic, for an adult.

Cyciohexamide - produces retroactive amnesia

Cylert - a type of speed

Datura, aka **Jimsonweed or thorn apple** - sometimes used to help a child conjure up their personal spirit

Iminodibenzyis - used for sedation

Lettuce Opium - traditional Hopi shaman trance drug

Mandrake - from the Mandragora plant, an ancient occult drug, a traditional witchcraft drug for causing people to sleep

Methaqualone - a rapid hypnotic drug that produces a dissociative high; it can be used to put someone into a coma

Pemoline-magnesium hydroxide, aka **PMH** - helps enhance conditioned avoidance training, by acting as a stimulant; is helpful for repetitive learning situations, by a general alerting effect on the mind

Phenothiazines - used to raise the threshold of electrical stimulation tolerance; to tranquilize or induce sleep

Rowan - traditional sleeping/death herb of witches; May Day is also called Rowan Tree Witch Day.

Seconal, aka **Seconal Sodium** or **Secobarbital Sodium** - a popular programming drug to stabilize programming; to set in deep programming into the base of the mind, such as dates and codes, and to block out memory of missions by slaves, see various paragraphs below for more explanations. Used in 10, 20, 30, 50, 100 mg. increments. A tubal pregnancy/birth can be hidden in a woman by 300-400 mg., while surgery on an adult man may require 500 mg.

Tetrodotoxin - made from the Puffer Blowfish; used by Voudoun and others to create a zombie state

* * * * * * * *

In our discussion of drugs used in programming, this chapter will expand upon the previous book, by discussing the application of drugs to:

a. stabilize the programming after torture
b. hiding the codes
c. building in deeply embedded structures and beliefs and the creation of false identities
d. to influence the memory by drugs; to stimulate instinctual behaviors
e. to create moods and attitudes, by synthetically manufacturing and injecting the brain's own natural amines.

Stabilizing the Programming

The total mind-control of the Illuminati is called "trauma-based mind-control," because repeated traumas are inflicted upon the victim in a very systematic, calculated, inhumane way. The tortures and stress are all parts of a programming package.

After a particular harsh session of programming, the victim's mind will be in a high state of terror, shock, dissociativeness and splintering. The victim's mind can't take much more, and the potential of having uncontrolled splintering of the victim's mind, and thereby having the destruction of the mind and programming, threatens the programmer's control. The programmer wants the mind and body to rest, so that the programming can set in, without destabilizing events occurring.

For instance, after severe water torture (drowning), the programmer will want the programming (hypnotic script) to set in, and he will give seconal (aka Seconal Sodium or Secobarbital Sodium) to induce a deep sleep. Sleep occurs within 10 to 15 minutes. Sometimes a victim's heart has been pushed to its limits during a trauma, and they must shut the body down, to let the victim rest. Seconal is a drug of choice for this.

Seconal is administered in hospitals or programming sites, where trained personnel know how to give the drug. Dirty psychiatrists, who understand the relationship between drugs and human behavior and who are either programmers themselves or assistants to programmers, often are the ones who give the victims drugs like Seconal.

Extensive Research Done to Influence Human Memory by Drugs

The complete list of researchers who have studied the effect drugs have on memory would require a massive book. However, we

Mind Control 101

will just mention a few that pertain to this book, briefly.

One of the places the effect of drugs on memory was researched was at the University of California at Irvine, CA. Another was at institutions in the Boston, Mass area, such as the Massachusetts General Hospital in Boston.

Dr. Talland in Boston tested the effects of PMH on human memory. He discovered PMH could help people relearn material that had been partially forgotten.

The Illuminati programmer, Cameron (aka Dr. White), also tried out various approaches, including the administration of RNA and RNA-synthesis stimulants.

John C. Lilly, who admits being a member of an Esoteric Mystery School, was a government researcher on the use of LSD to program people. He did part of his work on LSD programming at the Maryland Psychiatric Research Center, under admitted government financing. His book *Programming and Metaprogramming in the Human Biocomputer* (NY: Julian Press, 1967; revised format, 1972) is an excellent paper trail of how the Illuminati has used LSD to program total mind-controlled slaves. Originally, the book was given out only to a few select people. The book attempts to hide what it talks about behind a long intro, long sentences, big words and arcane psychological terms, but it does spell out how they do the mind-control programming with LSD. A section later in this chapter will lay out for the reader how they do this.

One Type of Experience of Victim Hypnotic Drug and Mind Control

The drugged victim feels like he is looking through a keyhole, and the hypnotic voice of the programmer is the key hole. The world may be very shadowy and drawn in on itself. The mind has its attention on the hypnotist/programmer.

The Basic Phases of Memory

The human memory process can be basically broken down into three phases - the registration phase, the retention phase and the retrieval phase. Great amount of research has gone into how to use drugs to manipulate each of those phases. Great amount of research also went into how to measure people's abilities to *learn, remember* and *do non-learned behavior,* such as arm-hand steadiness and visual time reaction.

What the Mind Control Programmers Use to Manipulate Memory

Scopolamine was found to impair short-term memory. It was discovered that retrograde amnesia could be created by electroshock, several hours after the brain had learned something. This lesson caused the Illuminati and those working in Mind Control with them to use cattle prods and stun guns.

If a person performed something they were to forget, they can be stunned or given Scopolamine to deaden their memory. A quick anesthetic applied immediately after something has been done might also impair the retention of what had happened.

Yet another way is Seconal, which will be discussed soon. Low doses of analeptic drugs given about 10 to 20 minutes before training were found to help learning. Analeptic drugs include bemegride, diazadamantanol, pentylenete-trazol, picotoxin, and strychnine.

It was discovered that strychnine helps enhance classical conditioning. It can be administered either before or after the learning has taken place. It is believed that memory storage is enhanced by strychnine and strychnine sulfate. Strychnine was also found to help protect the mind's memory against the effect of electroshock.

Abusers out on the street have been turning to GHB and Rohypnol, to decrease inhibitions and to cause memory loss in their victims. Rohypnol (which sells for up to $10 a tablet) is dependable but more expensive than the GHB.

A number of women who have been raped by adding these drugs to their alcoholic drinks at the Club Boca, Palm Beach, FL made the paper, after they were drugged and raped, after partying at the club. (The Palm Beach Post, Mar., 1996, pp. 1B, 10B.)

GHB (Gamma Hydroxy Butyrate) is a compound essential to the body. It acts similar to a neurotransmitter. It helps release the Human Growth Hormone and removes inhibitions around intimacy, as well as some other beneficial effects. GHB crosses the blood-brain barrier and metabolizes into GABA. GHB's high degree of safety was proven over 25 years of research and was basically an established fact, before the FDA and the media demonized GHB. Several sources seem to indicate that the FDA banned GHB - not because it has dangerous side effects, which it doesn't have, in spite of the established media's disinformation campaign with half-truths - but because it is not patented by the drug companies and would cut into their profits.

GHB also has a great aphrodisiac effect. It reduces inhibitions to have sex, but because the woman's clitoris is more sensitive, it interferes with female orgasms. However, when the women do achieve it, it is longer and more intense, according to GHB researchers. (This author got much information on GHB from the Centurion Aging Research Lab.)

GHB is described here, because it is a drug that is known by the type of people who use sexual slaves and other people, and its use and misuse pertain to Mind Control. Like so many things involved with mind-control, GHB and many other items could be put to positive uses, if used in the proper way.

Sometimes the programmers use drugs, rather than ECS (Electro Convulsive Shock), to destroy the memory in slaves, after they have done some mission for the Illuminati, the Syndicates or cult they belong to. The decision to use drugs, rather than ECS, is largely personal tastes. The very sadistic programmers enjoy using ECS, while the less sadistic ones often use the drugs, which in some instances actually perform better but are not as violent to the victim of Mind Control.

Retroactive amnesia can be caused by an intra-cerebral or a subcutaneous (under the skin) shot of Acetoxy-cycloheximide, cyclohexamide, or puromyxcin. A more sophisticated technique incorporates the drug Seconal (aka Seconal sodium), the victim's dissociativeness (the MPD), and hypnosis. Seconal is a strong sedative that puts people into sleep. The programmers have considered it "wonderful." The victim's mind is conditioned hypnotically to be able to remember the drugged- Seconal state. Then the hypnotic command is given that, if anything about a particular mission is remembered, the person will immediately trigger (pull-up to the front of the mind) the Seconal memory. This is why many therapists discover their clients getting sleepy, when they get close to certain thoughts or when they try to do therapeutic work.

The Power & Use of Symbols & Rituals for Mind Control

Rituals and symbols have incredible power over people. Rituals help define the people involved and how they think of themselves as part of the group. As a result, every culture has its own set of rituals and symbols.

These rituals include the obvious, like Jewish bar mitzvahs and Catholic confirmations and graduation celebrations. Amid all the rituals of our lives are also the less obvious rituals, like passing your first drivers test or getting your first apartment.

The purpose of a ritual is to bring the participants more fully into the society or subculture and thus help them to more easily conform to the regulations of that group.

Think of each ritual as a way to mark a significant turning point in the person's life.

In his book and video series, *The Power of Myth,* Joseph Campbell describes how symbols have a simplifying effect that all the members of the group can link to a specific meaning. The rituals that are created around these symbols give each participant a personal experience, something visceral, an NLP "anchor" to the symbol and its meaning.

Rituals and their related symbols help define the reality of the group. As it relates to Mind Control, the more a controller can incorporate rituals into the experience of his/her subjects, the more deeply the prescribed reality is accepted.

Example of Rituals and Mind Control

In the early days of America, many social organizations were established. Many of them had very little more than mens' clubs, with no real social or political agenda. One of those organizations, which took root in the southern United States, was the Ku Klux Klan, better known as the KKK.

The KKK had its share of rituals from the beginning. When racial tensions began to grow in the American south, the KKK took it up as a personal cause. They combined their rituals, complete with colorful wardrobe, burning crosses and vows of secrecy, to put emphasis on the superiority of whites over blacks and immigrants.

Anything can be used to implement rituals and symbols for Mind Control. To do it, consider what the message is you want your subject to receive and the reality you want them to value. Your message may also include the beliefs you wish to instill.

Let's start with the symbols. Take a look at all the symbols in your life. They are everywhere. Crosses, pentagrams, stars, company logos, team uniforms, fraternity paddles, corporate T-shirts and caps, hair styles, tennis shoes, images of heroes and deities, TV stars, gurus and prophets. Symbols are everywhere. It is the rituals that give these symbols meaning.

Rituals and symbols are obvious in religions. They are also present in politics.

From the Solidarity Movement, to Ronald Regan's presidential campaign and rise of the Nazi party, the historical displays of patriotism and national unity have employed symbols and rituals. The rituals take the form of rallies. The symbols - banners, leaders and flags.

The same is often true for corporate environments.

For the operator who seeks to employ this knowledge of symbols and ritual, a little creativity is all it takes. The symbols can be preexisting or created. The more the rituals include heightened emotional states and secrecy, the more powerful the impact on the participants.

Psychic Influence

Psychic influence is the ability to effect people's moods or behavior, by mere thought. It is a field of parapsychology, along the lines of telepathy and mind reading and has been explored scientifically by both the academic and military communities.

The academic goals of these types of studies is to measure and understand if psychic influence is possible.

The military seeks to use psychic influence to effect people for political gain.

Most academic studies on the subject have proven very little, with only a very small percentage of experiments giving any indication that psychic influence is possible. That has not discouraged those who want to explore psychic influence on a personal level.

For that reason, the information presented here on psychic influence relies less on scientific evidence and more on a consensus of testimonials from people who have reported some control over psychic influence.

One of the factors that's unique to psychic influence, as opposed to other forms of Mind Control, is that a large quantity of "work" is done to and on the controller. This is because the controller's personal beliefs can dramatically affect the success or failure of any psychic influence experiments.

Let's address these beliefs and how they are conceptualized by the controller.

The Belief in Connection

One belief that prevents people from effectively influencing others on the psychic level is the belief that there is a separation that prevents anything other than influence through the senses.

Imagine that the senses are nothing more than filters that limit what you can perceive. The eyes only perceive visible light; the ears only perceptible sound waves; and the physical body is limited to heat, vibration and touch. These add to the belief that there is nothing more to perceive beyond that and that we are, in fact, separate from one another.

So what if those senses and their limitations were eliminated? A simple conclusion is that, even though we perceive separation, on a deeper level, it does not exist.

If this were the case, it could be just as easy to find a way to connect via an extrasensory method. By reprogramming and removing the belief that psychic influence is not possible, the limitations that are contained by the belief itself are removed. At the very least ,the removal of these limitations create an opportunity to explore and test any theories of psychic influence.

Experimentation

In experimenting to get psychic influence, anything can be used, with the single outcome in mind to cause someone to do something, without sensory contact.

What follows are the types of experiments that the sender can practice.

Mind Control 101

Will

"Will" experiments are simply a matter of causing someone to do something from a distance, by energizing, forcing and propelling the action into the receiver, by thinking about it and "willing" it to occur.

An example of this would be that of sitting in a crowd of people and focusing on one individual, attempting to cause a behavior, like scratching the head, going to the bathroom, pulling the ear.

Imagination Exercises

Silva Mind Control is perhaps one known system of using imagination exercises for psychic influence. Imagination exercises for psychic influence usually include the sender imagining connecting with the receiver and delivering the message.

The imagination exercise is a meditative or self-hypnotic process, in which the sender/operator mentally imagines first, the connection to the receiver and the message or new behavior being transmitted and received.

Here is an example of a psychic influence exercise:

It is recommended that this exercise is done at a time when the subject is sleeping and in a mentally receptive state.

State your intention. For example, "Joe Smith will call me tomorrow, before noon." Close your eyes, and go through a relaxation or self-hypnosis process. When in "state," imagine lifting up out of your body and moving to a realm beyond the senses, where all things are connected. Reach out with your hands, as if "parting the veil," and imagine grasping Joe Smith in a sleeping state, while you move your hands accordingly.

With your hands, grab Joe and "unzip" him, as if he were a suit, and then put him on like a wet suit. When you have a good fit, walk Joe through the thoughts, emotions and actions of Joe making the call to you. When the exercise is complete, take off the "Joe suit," and zip him back up, and send him back through the void.

Next, imagine a golden messenger orb that holds your intention, "Joe will call me tomorrow, before noon," and instruct it to follow Joe and invade his thoughts, day dreams and impulses. When the sphere is completed with the intention and instructions, send it off into the void.

Once complete, end the imagination exercise with laughter.

The final instruction of ending the exercise with laughter is done to banish the thought from the sender's mind. This is done in the belief that having a conscious awareness of the exercise acts as an obstacle to successful results.

Ritual

The use of rituals to change the thoughts and actions of others has been used ever since the first love spell and curses were cast.

For several reasons, when using rituals to effect psychic influence, often intention is simplified into a phrase like a mantra or a symbol, called a *sigil*. This has several benefits. First, it only has meaning to the sender and protects them from other people knowing their intention. Second, it is easier to forget. This is important, because it is often believed that a conscious knowledge of the intention can be an obstacle to success.

There are so many resources that list these rituals of influencing others that they won't be mentioned here. All one has to do is rent a few horror videos to get the idea. So without going into the depth of what to do as a ritual of psychic influence, it is safe to say that ritual is a form of theater; that is done for the participants and by the participants, with an outcome of effecting the subject.

Rituals of psychic influence will tend to involve the participants doing a pre-designed theatrical performance, with the hopes of becoming so involved in the part that they are playing, that the "energy" effects the intended subject. Often the participants will portray a magician, who summons a spirit or a god, who is casting divine influence over the intended subject.

Many writers on the topic of psychic influence consider any attempt to influence someone in this manner as "black magic." That is not a judgment suited for this book, as our only concern is what works.

Dreams

The ability to contact and influence people in their dreams is difficult, at best. To do so, most people have to overcome some deeply ingrained habits that cause us to minimize and forget what we've dreamed.

The first efforts to gain any skill of dream control and dream influence is to remember dreams and then to control them. After being able to consistently remember their dreams, the control must then be able to control them and become aware they are dreaming, while they are dreaming. This lucid dreaming process is best documented by the works of author Stephen Le Berge, in his book *Lucid Dreaming* and subsequent works.

As the operator masters lucid dreaming, they can attempt to direct themselves into the dreamscape of the person they are trying to influence.

Influence by way of Ecstatic/Inhibitory States

For the controller who has a clear intention for the subject that they wish to send psychically, it is often prescribed that they enter an extreme mental/emotional state, in order to "charge" the message.

The extremes can take two forms: *inhibitory* or *ecstatic*. Inhibitory states include any state where the senses are closed down. This can include a hypnotic state or prolonged sessions of sensory deprivation. Another example of this extreme inhibitory state is the "death posture," where the sender attempts to close off every bodily function, including breathing, until the very last moment, when they think of and "charge" their intention.

Examples of ecstatic states for charging these intentions are dancing, chanting, spinning, prolonged sexual activity, all done while the intention is held in mind. Often when using ecstatic/inhibitory states to charge an intention, the intention is reduced to a phrase or sigil, as mentioned above.

Drugs

A disclaimer here is important. First, drugs are dangerous, and using them in this culture to "psychically influence" someone is an act that invites the potential of straitjackets and rubber rooms. Nonetheless, it's been tried.

Peruvian shamans have claimed to do this using the hallucinogenic tea ayahuasca.

It is safe to say that, if anyone wants to attempt such an act, this is not going to be an instructional source on how to do it. One must be of stable mind and character and best have an experienced guide, who is familiar with the effects of these drugs and how to guide someone through the psychological mine fields they present.

Final Note on Psychic Influence

Mind Control 101

As for using psychic influence, there are no hard and fast rules. Many have preceded you in the research in this field, but as a general rule, the only thing you will discover consistently is that everyone discovers their own best way of doing it.

As the sender practices these experiments in combinations and variations of them, they will develop an understanding of what gets the best results for them.

Other Techniques of Mind Control
Cunning Acts of Guile and Trickery of Cults and Con-Men

By studying con-men, one can discover just how easy it is for people to be convinced that something is real. The downside of this field of study is that it can create a painful sense of conscious in someone with a firm set of morals and ethics. Nonetheless, it is a field of study that has some good information in it.

Remember, to be good at Mind Control, you don't have to do anything in this book. Just learn.

High Frequency Directional Voice Projection

It is amazing what can come to you, when you are watching The Discovery Channel.

There exists a technology that's used by the government and is now available for commercial use that consists of flat speakers that project a sound, much like a laser projects light. It works by using ultra high frequency sound waves of millions of cycles per second. Normally, the human ear can hear from between 20 to 50,000 cycles per second of sound, but these sound waves are manipulated, so that they are very audible and focused into narrow a beam that can only be heard by the person who is in the line of sight of the speaker.

To my knowledge, using this to convince people they are hearing voices has never been proposed until now, but the effect would be quite dramatic - even more dramatic, if this devise were used on people who already had a history of auditory hallucinations, such as schizophrenics.

Scientology TRs

Scientology has a so-called communications course that is the basic introduction to the religion called "The Training Routines" or TRs for short. It is also the first step into the Scientology indoctrination process. The Scientology TRs can be easily found by doing a search on the internet.

Like any good Mind Control process, it starts off based on a fact that is true for most people; that when we try to communicate with others, we tend to be more concerned with our own problems and objectives than truly "being" with that person. This fact, the Scientologists will tell you, is what prevents us from being able to communicate well and get what we want.

How it presents this and helps to resolve that problem is through an ingenious series of exercises that eventually lead the student into the trap of doing whatever the instructor asks them to do.

The TRs are presented in a "gradient" or series of steps, with each successive TR building on previous ones. This is an ideal example of "indoctrinated knowledge," used by religions all over the world, in which one can't learn secret 'D,' unless they have successively learned secrets 'A' through 'C,' first.

The beginning TRs are simple enough. Two students are asked to face each other, knee to knee, and to look at each other, without expression. In Scientology terms, they are supposed to "be in the moment" with that person. This, by itself, can be very uncomfortable for most people, and nervous laughter often results. If either of them begin to laugh, giggle or look away in discomfort, the other student is instructed to shout "Flunk!" and describe what occurred "Laughing!" and then restart the TR with "Begin!"

After some practice, sometimes hours, the students learn to very comfortably look at the other person and "be in the moment" with them.

The gradient continues to other seemingly innocuous TRs and then to a harder step called "Bull Baiting," in which the students take turns trying to provoke any response from their partner. Their partner, in the mean time, is trying not to laugh, get angry or be insulted, while just sitting there receiving whatever verbal cajoling or abuse that's offered.

This, in itself, has great value, because it teaches people to be their most calm in the midst of huge external one-on-one pressure. Those who have gone through these TRs report that it gives them a calmness of mind, enough to think rationally under extreme pressure, and the exercise itself often creates a sense of accomplishment and a high for the successful participant. Combine that with the positive feedback from the instructors ,and the student is very eager to do more.

Ultimately, as they go through the gradient of TRs, they are taught about what's called the "Tone 40" scale. The Tone 40 is a scale of aliveness; on the low end is depression and death; on the high end is the ability to say something and make it come about, by the sheer power of its delivery. Students are taught to look at an ashtray and tell it forcefully to "Stand up!"

Doing this for a long enough period of time, the student becomes convinced that their will can be delivered through their voice, to cause the ashtray to "Stand up!" even when they reach with their hand and make it "stand up."

Lastly, they are given the final TR and told to use the Tone 40 voice with each other, giving simple orders like, "Stand up! "Thank you." "Walk to the door!" "Stop!" "Thank you." "Walk to me!" "Stop!" and so on. The process goes on for over an hour,with each person taking turns as the controller and the subject. They are essentially learning how to respond to orders without questioning.

This is where the devious part of this process occurs that no one who takes part is aware of. By going all the way through this process to this final Tone 40 TR the students of this class are training each other to respond to the Scientologists when they tell them "John, Stand up. This is Sarah. Sarah take John to the registration desk and sign John up for the auditing!"

The conditioning is so thorough its almost impossible to resist the commands that are given.

Forcing Choice as in Psychological Card Forces

In card magic that uses slight of hand, there is a whole list of tricks that fall under the category of "card forces."

To force a card means to offer a person a chance to pick a card, and force them to pick a specific card, while they believe they have completely free choice. Most of these forces use some form of slight of hand. One magic book made a list of over one hundred different forms of card forces, and it was just scratching the surface.

Some magicians have fine tuned this by using a psychological force that compels people to choose a specific card, merely by choosing the right words to say. For example, by asking a person to think of a card, and "make the colors bright and vivid," the person will tend to only include red cards. By telling them to imagine the card with sharp contrasts, black cards will imagined.

This ideal, that choices can be forced like cards, opens up a whole field of possibilities in Mind Control and causes one to examine the seemingly mundane things that effect the illusion of choice.

The Power of the Emotional Chamber

The Emotional Chamber is a sales and seduction technique that was described by persuasion author JD Fuentes, in his book, "Sexual Key." It dives deep into archetypes and patterns that are specific to women, that can effect how they perceive things and make choices about them, including products and partners.

To easily understand it, think of sex, and then turn it into a metaphor of feelings leading to a decision.

There are several components to the emotional chamber:
* A pleasant emotion that initiates the decision making
* An invitation to let it come inside and be felt
* A feeling, color or sound is given to the emotion
* A building up of that emotion, which brings forth another emotion
* An invitation to bring that new emotion in, along with its physical feelings
* The cycle can continue on with a cycle of one emotion after another being invited inside, feelings felt, building up and culminating and yielding to another emotion.

If it isn't obvious, this is a metaphor for a female sexual orgasm.

For the sake of example, the decision will be to buy a widget. Using the Emotional Chamber process, it would sound like this:

When you think of the widget, one thing that you can become aware of is a feeling of interest. So when you notice that interest, it is like you've created an opening for it. Letting it come inside, so you notice the electric tingling that brings it to your attention, and as that feeling of interest builds stronger and stronger, more and more, you may begin to notice another feeling... curiosity... so you bring that curiosity in, and take it in very deep. And like anything you are curious about that you take in, you want to know more and more about it, and that firm feeling just grows firmer and firmer, until you finally have a welcomed understanding that you can use this widget. A smooth, fluid acceptance that this is yours to use anytime you want....

Of course, the cycle of the emotional chamber can be repeated again and again.

MKULTRA

MK-ULTRA was the name of a secret government project that was obsessively dedicated to the subject of Mind Control. The project was not limited by ethics or the laws of the government. Keep in mind that MK-ULTRA occurred during the time of the Cold War, when all of the nation was feeling under the hammer of nuclear war by the "communist menace." The U. S. government feared and suspected the worst; namely that communist nations were creating Mind Controlled Manchurian candidates or "sleeper agents," that could be triggered to do any act of terror at any time. Their only recourse was to develop their own form of Mind Control.

What they came upon was research done in Nazi Germany that indicated people who grew up under traumatic childhoods made excellent candidates for this type of research. The result is what is called "Trauma Based Mind Control," in which, allegedly, children have been intentionally raised and abused to create the ideal agent - an agent that will do anything asked, even suicide or murder, without question, and have no memory of the act when completed.

MKULTRA – Cathy O'Brian and Mark Phillips
Disclaimer

This topic you will read about is NOT a form of Mind Control that is endorsed by this book, the author or anyone known to the author.

The book, "The Trance-Formation of America," By Cathy O'Brian and Mark Phillips contains a description of what was alleged to have happened to one person ,under the clandestine supervision of the U. S. government. The details of the story are shocking and include accusations of secret black ops projects that institutionalize child sexual abuse and trauma, based Mind Control procedures, for the purpose of creating a secret government "über-agent," who will follow every command to the letter, and have no memory their actions.

Of course, the government has never confirmed these accusations, and they could easily be dismissed as sensationalism, if it were not for the incredible detail of the story and the lingering thought that a secret government agency could do such a thing.

As a study in Mind Control, it bares examination.

The story of Cathy O'Brian begins with her earliest memory of being repeatedly sexually abused by her father. According to her, undergoing that intensity of abuse at such an early age forced her mind to create different personalities, to deal with the trauma. This is what is clinically called "Disassociative Personality Disorder" (DPD) and has been previously called multiple or split personality disorder. Someone who has DPD will have several personalities that act independently of each other, and therefore memories of actions by one personality are not recalled by other personalities.

As the story continued, her photo was spotted in child pornography by a secret arm of the U. S. government. She was then "purchased" from her father, so that she could be trained to serve in government black operations. Her responsibilities were largely to have sex with whomever she was instructed to, for the purposes of government bribery or blackmail. She would also be enlisted to act as courier for money, drugs and information from one underground government operation to another.

The nature of her DPD made her ideal for the job. Because of a childhood of constant fear and threat, people who are diagnosed with DPD tend to have a very heightened sensory acuity, that gives them the skills of photographic memory.

Because people with DPD are already able to compartmentalize experiences, Cathy's handlers used a combination of hypnosis and torture to create further compartments, that would allow them to hide precise instructions within her memory, to be revealed when the proper trigger word was given. The hypnotic training was so thorough that these compartments even hid the information from Cathy, herself.

A further benefit is that, since one personalty can be called on after another, no one personality knows how long the host has been awake and without sleep, so they tend to have boundless energy.

According to Cathy O'Brian, people who became these types of agents had no idea of any other possible life. They knew their value as a person was zero. Following the orders given to them resulted in a life of sexual exploitation, abuse and fear; this was all that they knew, and they followed them to the letter. They were often "eliminated" by the time they were 30 years old, because their minds would often begin to integrate memories and begin to learn to think autonomously.

A book that details this form of trauma based Mind Control is *Deeper Insights into the Illuminati Formula,* by Fritz Springmeier and Cisco Wheeler and can be found on the internet and ordered from book stores. The book has a very strong Christian bias and heavy overtones of conspiracy theories but is full of detail about the procedures of trauma-based Mind Control.

Cult Mind Control Tactics & Strategies

Stephen Hassan, author of *Combating Cult Mind Control* describes the model of cult Mind Control, with the acronym B.I.T.E., which stands for control over Behavior, Information, Thoughts and Emotions.

Keep in mind that each of these, or at least components of much of these, can be used in many ways to lead someone to the outcome you desire.

Behavior Control

Behavior Control is described as the regulation of one's physical and mental reality. A new recruit is encouraged repeatedly to squelch his/her critical-thinking skills and gut instincts, in return for group approval and inclusion. Exerting such a control over people allows high-pressure groups to determine most or all of the following:

* Where, how and with whom recruits live and associate.
* What clothing, colors and hairstyles to wear.
* Which foods/drinks are accepted or rejected.
* How much financial dependence recruits are to have on the group; what percentage of recruits' income is collected for the

group's purposes.
* How much time is spent on leisure activities, such as relaxing, sleeping and vacationing.

Once behavior control is put into effect, recruits respond and react accordingly. The recruits:

* Unwittingly commit themselves to the required indoctrination sessions and group rituals.
* Relinquish many personal decision-making processes, and go to the group to determine minor and/or major life decisions.
* Are required to report all doubts about the group, perceived negative thoughts, personal feelings and external activities to their superiors.
* Undergo endless cycles of verbal and/or physical abuse, then being praised or rewarded. (When husbands do that to wives, it is called the "battered wife syndrome.)
* Steer clear of individualism and independent thought as group-thought prevails.
* Adhere to often unforeseen rigid rules and regulations.
* Develop a need for obedience to and dependency on the group

Information Control in cults can involve six key elements:
1) Deception
2) Outside Information Forbidden
3) Levels of Information
4) Spying and Surveillance
5) Group Propaganda
6) Unconfidential Confessions

1) Deception
Cult members will often:
* Deliberately withhold information from recruits
* Distort information to make it appear acceptable
* Lie to obtain their goal

2) Outside Information Forbidden
Access to information outside of that of the group is minimized or discouraged. These restrictions are set on:
* Certain books, articles, newspapers, magazines, TV and radio shows, that expose the group

* Critical information pertaining to the internal problems within the group
* Written critiques, letters, editorials or history of involvements of former members of the group

3) Levels of Information

Often, and necessarily so within cults, information is compartmentalized. That is, only certain top-notch members are privy to exactly what is happening in the leadership and with the group, as a whole. Information pertaining to the group doctrine is fed in small, digestible spoonfuls to new recruits for a reason - so that they remain ignorant, for the time being, of the workings of the system. Leaders are seen as possessing what Lifton called "sacred science" or having the ability to decipher and interpret doctrines, philosophies, etc, in a way that no one else has ever done or could ever do.

* Information is not freely accessible
* Information varies at different levels and missions within a pyramid
* Leadership decides who "needs to know" what

4) Spying and Surveillance

* Pairing up with "buddy" system to monitor and control
* Reporting deviant thoughts, feelings, and actions to leadership

5) Group Propaganda

* Newsletters, magazines, journals, audio tapes, videotapes, etc.
* Misquotations, statements taken out of context from non-cult sources

6) Unconfidential Confessions

* Information about "sins" is used to abolish identity boundaries.
* Past "sins" are used to manipulate and control; no forgiveness or absolution is given.

Thought Control

Here are a few guidelines for thought control:
* Need to internalize the group's doctrine as "the truth".
* Map = Reality
* "All-or-none" mentality
* Good against evil

* Us against them (inside versus outside)
* Adopt "loaded" language (characterized by "thought-terminating cliches").

Words are the tools we use to think with. These "special" words constrict rather than expand understanding. They function to reduce complexities of experience into trite, platitudinous "buzz words," "thought-terminating cliches" and simplistic slogans, to stop critical thinking.

Even the self-help community has its list of loaded lingo, with things like "shame spiral," "stinkin' thinking," "shoulding on yourself." Only "good" and "proper" thoughts are encouraged.

Practice thought-stopping techniques, prevent "reality testing," by stopping "negative" thoughts and allowing only "good" thoughts, and prohibit rational analysis, critical thinking and constructive criticism:

* Denial, rationalization, justification and wishful thinking.
* Chanting, meditating, praying.
* Speaking in "tongues."
* Singing or humming.
* Only "good" and "proper" thoughts are encouraged.
* No critical questions about the leader, doctrine, or policy are seen as legitimate.
* No alternative belief systems are viewed as legitimate, good or useful (exclusivity).

Emotional Control

Emotional control allows cults to manipulate and narrow the range of a recruit's feelings. The objective of cults is to make recruits think that any doubts about the group is their fault and never that of the leader(s) or the group. Any negativism toward the group is often misdirected back to the recruit, causing the recruit to internalize their doubts.

This section contains the following:
1) Guilt Association
2) Fear Induction
3) Extremism
4) Phobia Indoctrination

1) Guilt Association

Mind Control 101

Cults induce large amounts of guilt, typically in association with the following:

* Who you are (and why you are not living up to your potential)

* Who your family is (those from dysfunctional families are to attribute their dysfunctional past to their not being a member of the group yet; those from well-adjusted families are to feel guilty for having had it so good)

* What secrets lie in your past (sexual history, childhood mistakes, any past criminal involvement is overly emphasized)

* With whom you are affiliated (the company you keep, boyfriend/girlfriend/fiancees shunned; family, friends, etc.)

* What you think (how you feel and what you do about your feelings, whether what you think and feel is acceptable to the group)

* Social guilt (recruit is made to feel inadequate, because of his/her social status)

* Historical guilt (recruit is forced to take on the oppression of his/her ancestors and the plight of martyred persons)

2) Fear Induction

In order for guilt induction to successfully operate, cults must be able to instill fear in their followers:

* Fear of thinking independently. (Recruits wonder whether they are making right decisions, what the consequences will be if they think independently.)

* Fear of the "outside" world. (Recruits have a "we/they" mentality, and generally see all in the group as "saved," while all outside the group are "lost.")

* Fear of enemies. (Recruits are indoctrinated to be very paranoid of all those on the outside, including the government, cult awareness groups and/or society in general.)

* Fear of losing salvation. (Recruits are taught that salvation is attained only through group affiliation and nowhere else.)

* Fear of being shunned. (Recruits often risk losing family, friends, job, etc., if they decide to leave. Many cults "mark" or otherwise collectively shun former members.)

* Fear of disapproval. (Recruits learn to live according to the laws of the leaders, and learn that deviating from these laws is detrimental to the well-being of both oneself and the others in the

group.)

3) Extremism

Cults often deal in extremes. Here are a few examples of extremism in cults:

* Extremes of emotional highs and lows (rewards and punishments go hand-in-hand)
* Ritual and often public confessions of sins (confessions provoked and exaggerated by inductor, i.e. a recruit who confesses to having had a few beers is labelled "an alcoholic.")
* "We/they" mentality, in which group sees itself as better than the rest of the world, The group sees itself as the only people capable of accurate doctrinal interpretation (also called "sacred science").

Phobia Indoctrination

Phobia indoctrination is the programming of irrational fears of ever leaving the group, or even questioning the leadership's authority. Recruits are manipulated to the extent that they cannot visualize a positive and successful future, without being in the group. They are taught that horrific consequences will ensue, if they are to leave (i.e., "hell," "demon possession," accidents, suicide and/or insanity, etc.).

Often, former cult members are so confused upon leaving that the group's predictions become a self-fulfilling prophecy. Many former cult members have killed themselves, because that was exactly what the group said they would do. Those who leave are often shunned and rejected by the group. From the group perspective, there is never a legitimate reason to leave. Those who leave are perceived as "weak," "undisciplined," "unspiritual," "worldly," "brainwashed by family, friends, counselors" and/or seduced by the world of drugs, sex and rock-and-roll.

Comments on B.I.T.E. Cult Mind Control Model

Not all of these components of cult Mind Control are needed to effectively influence someone. Many smaller parts of this description are used in everyday situations of influence.

In the area of behavior control, a salesperson, for example, will limit the choices of chairs a prospect can sit in, and then tell him to only sit in one chair. This can also be done by limiting the hours a person can be contacted.

Artful Mind Control is best done by avoiding the negative aspects of the B.I.T.E. Model. While abuse and coercion are certainly usable aspects of Mind Control, they are by no means essential to creating a compliant Mind Control subject.

The 5 Steps of Mind Control Outlined by Edgar H. Schein

His five criteria for a person's "changing" or conforming to the group norm are:
1) New identification
2) Behavior modification
3) Mystical manipulation
4) Mind-altering techniques
5) Confession eliciting.

This is a brief description of each of them:

1) New Identification

A new "cult identity" is created and imposed formally in indoctrination sessions, as well as informally through personal relations with cult members, tapes, books on group doctrines.

For the controller, this is an opportunity to consider the type of identity you want your subject to take on.

2) Behavior Modification Techniques

Behavior modification techniques include the reward/punishment cycle, the use of thought-stopping techniques, and the control of environment.

3) Mystical Manipulation

Mystical manipulation is the perception of coincidental or inevitable events as spiritual signs. Recruits are trained that such signs are symbols of the greatness of the group.

The controller can either create a mystical event through guile, or simply use events that happen naturally, and give them meaningful interpretations for his subject.

4) Mind-altering Techniques

Hypnosis, repetition, monotony and rhythm are often used to numb the thought processes of recruits. These are often carried out through excessive chanting, praying, decreeing and visions.

5) Eliciting Confession

Testimonials and/or confessions are forcibly and continually extracted from recruits, as a means of keeping recruits dependent and obedient.

This process is seldom used in a constructive fashion, like it should. Usually it creates guilt and shame to motivate the subject to change. A more positive use of confession is one that is followed by acceptance, instead of guilt. This acceptance will bind the subject closer to the controller, as in the Prodigal Son pattern mentioned earlier in this book.

How to Create a Recovered Memory

In the late 1980s, there were a litany of reports of people who recovered repressed memories of childhood abuse. Some of these reports were shocking and included memories of participation in human sacrifices, satanic rituals and sexual abuse from family members; the discovery of multiple personalities, not to mention alien abduction. These memories were detailed and elaborate, and the subjects were convinced of their authenticity, even when evidence contradicted them.

This phenomenon quickly became known as "recovered memory syndrome," and a slew of psychologists gained a great deal of acclaim and authority at helping people uncover these lost and dangerous memories. The therapists were so convinced that these memories were repressed from the conscious mind that the evidence of the repression was the fact that they weren't remembered.

What came of these "recovered memories?"

In spite of the publicity (reporter, Geraldo Reveria even made an hour-long special report), the official investigations found there was no evidence of these events having ever taken place - and another discovery took place, that memories and even alternate personalities could be created and implanted, and the term "recovered memory" quickly became "implanted memory."

This is something that could be of great interest to anyone interested in Mind Control.

The interesting part of this discovery is that these false memories were created unintentionally by seemingly well-meaning psychologists, who assumed they were doing work to help people.

So the question is - what did they do to create this effect, so that a Mind Controller could duplicate it? Upon examination, there were several components of the work that these therapists did that created these false memories.

Conviction of the Therapist

Whether intentional or not if the controller or counselor portrays the belief that there are hidden memories within someone and rapport exists then the doorway is open to create false memories. The controller must act congruently with the belief that false memories exist.

The Misinformation Effect

The misinformation effect occurs when something factual is reported or demonstrated, and then other facts about it are introduced, which are not true.

For example, showing a video of a car accident and later asking the subject to describe the street signs in the video. The truth is that no street signs were in the video. A significant number of the people in this experience began to detail street signs that were not there.

Imagination Inflation

Studies have shown that when a person is asked to simply imagine they were taking part in an event, they would most likely accept that it really happened.

Repetition

Quite simply, the more the process of "recovering memories" is done, the easier it is for the subject to believe that it happened.

Conditioning

Rewarding the subject will improve the results. The simplest reward is the best; giving the subject attention and acknowledgment.

Putting this all together in some systematic fashion, the process could work as follows:

The controller would begin a discussion of how we learn from memories, and elicit various memories from the subject. The subject is rewarded by listening and through encouragement.

The next step is an "imagination exercise" aka hypnosis, of

reliving the memory, so that information can be used from the memory to be augmented and modified later. Other imagination exercises are incorporated that are not memories, but incorporate aspects of the subject's memory. The purpose is to ease the subject into confusing the two experiences.

During the imagination exercises (aka hypnosis), the controller can elicit from the subject the aspects of memory (NLP sub-modalities, for example) that make the memory real and believable. This can then be incorporated in any future sessions.

Allow some time to pass, a few days is enough, and talk about the aspects of the suggestions that were given that are not part of the memory, and elicit the values and meanings of those aspects. Once again use an imagination exercise to strengthen the impact of the implanted (false) aspects of the memory, and reinforce it with discussion.

Allowing time to pass between each meeting will further confuse the suggested aspects of the memory with the actual memory, itself.

Mind Tricks with Others

Mind Tricks is a category of fun, weird, short-term, interesting tricks one can do with others. They are tricks which can be very impressive when they work and will give the user the immediate reward of learning that there are amazing things that can be done with the mind.

Please note that sometimes they work - and sometimes they don't. The good news is that you have noting to lose, and they are a lot of fun.

How to Disassociate Yourself From Your Mistake

You are getting this one first, because this is the simplest and easiest mind trick there is.

It is also one of the most useful.

Let's assume, while in a conversation with someone, you say something that shocks or insults them. The reaction they give and look on their face will be obvious; you said something wrong.

Normally, we would backtrack and apologize, minimize or rationalize the comment, in order to appease the other person and calm them down. The problem with that is that it only brings attention to the insult.

The mind trick that resolves it is so simple, you will laugh.

All you do is step to one side, point to where you were just standing, and say with equal shock or insult, "Oh my God. I can NOT believe he just said that!"

The response you will get is one of laughter and amusement. The process works by unconsciously disassociating you from "the other guy," who said the shocking words.

When doing this, there is an important point to remember; that is to not refer back to your shocking comment, as it will relink you to the feelings those words elicited. Also, don't step back into the place that you were pointing to, as it might unconsciously relink you to the words you said.

This can also be done over the phone by simply saying, with shock, "Did he say what I thought he said? I can't believe he said that!"

The Tilted Register

Imagine asking the clerk for more change than you actually have coming ... and they give it to you!

This one is very sneaky, and if you are in a tight spot for money, it might work for you. Those who've tried it find that there is nothing to lose in doing it and that it will work from 10% to 30% of the time, when the conditions are right.

First, let's understand something about the mind; namely, that it can only do a very limited number of things at one time. Scientists call it the "seven plus or minus two," meaning, at the most, our minds can concentrate on five to nine things at one time. If we are given more information than we can handle or too many things to do at one time, our mind "locks up." At that moment, anything that is told to us slips past our conscious mind and is only heard by the unconscious mind.

If we can create this "lock up" of the mind in someone, we can use it to give a suggestion to the unconscious mind. Granted, it doesn't always work. When it doesn't, no big deal, nothing is lost. When it does work... WOW! People will do things that you never thought possible.

Here is how to do "The Tilted Register."

Mind Control 101

The controller would buy something at a store for less than a dollar and cordially greet the clerk, and give him a five dollar bill. As the clerk rings up the purchase and the cash drawer is open, the controller points to the register and says, "Is your register tipping over? Just give me a ten, and keep the change. It looks like it wobbles a bit when the drawer opened."

The key to making this work is in the timing. The controller needs to be quite aware of when the clerk is most distracted-looking at the register. So when the controller says, "Is your register tipping over?" he will wait to see that the clerk is paying attention to the register and not to the counting of change. The controller then follows with, "Just give me a ten, and keep the change. It looks like it wobbles a bit when the drawer opened." These last two sentences must flow evenly, in the same tone of voice, as if they are both about the same topic. The controller then simply waits for the change to be delivered and sees if the clerk hands him the ten dollar bill.

Other than walking off with the money, there are few other things that can happen.

* The clerk notices the suggestion. The controller simply shakes his head and makes a disparaging comment about "the new math."

* The clerk gives the ten dollars and then realizes the mistake. The controller simply acknowledges the mistake and acts just as confused as the clerk.

If you try this enough, you will begin to notice the type of people who will most likely follow through with your suggestion. They will tend to be running on automatic at the register and be in a sort of "cashiers trance"

The Russian Game

This is the name of a con-game that is pure Mind Control trickery. It was demonstrated on the BBC by performer Derren Brown, and there are several places on the internet where you can see it.

The essences of The Russian Game is where the controller asks for directions from a stranger; they also give him their wallet, cell phone and wrist watch, as well... just because they were asked!

Like the Tilted Register, this will work only on about a third of the people it's tried on.

To do this, the controller would go to an area that is frequented by both tourists and locals alike. He would stand with an open map in his hands and a bottle of water, along with a confused and lost look on his face. Waiting for someone to pass by, the controller is looking, ideally, for someone walking by who is in their own "walking trance."

"Excuse me. Can you... give me ... the directions to Market Street?" (Looking at map and pointing, the controller gets the information from the passer-by. By doing this, it creates some confusion in the subject as to what to really focus on. This is key in this process.)

"So it is down and to the left and two blocks... you don't mind giving me that, do you? Great, thank you." (The controller extends his hand to shake the hand of the helpful citizen, then puts the water bottle in the hand of the passer by.) "Here, could you hold this? (The controller pats his pockets, as if looking for something). And could you hand me your wallet? Yes, that's good... Oh, do you have a cell phone? Great! Thank you. So it is just left and two blocks...oh... and my drink... That's right?" The controller then walks away, with all the passer-by has given him.

Of course, this sounds so absurd that no one can think that it is that simple, but it is, and it will work about 10% to 30% of the time. This depends largely on picking the right person to approach. That can only be learned by experience.

The Handshake Interrupt

The Handshake Interrupt is unique in hypnosis, as a way to covertly induce confusion and introduce a suggestion, by just a hand shake.

Before going into how to do the Handshake Interrupt, it is a good idea to understand how it works.

To understand it, first let's consider the common everyday handshake. We do it all the time and don't ever give it a second thought. We've done it so often that it is thought of as one, single, smooth motion, when in fact it is several motions performed one right after the other, in such a smooth and fluid way, we forget the steps that make it up.

Steps to the Ordinary Handshake

Mind Control 101

1. Extend right hand by bending the elbow to a right angle
2. Palm facing left
3. Move arm forward
4. Reach for right hand of other person
5. With right hand, grab the other person's right hand, interlocking the thumbs on top and fingers grabbing lower part of hand
6. Move hands up and down
7. Separate hands
8. This is usually accompanied with direct eye contact and smile or expression of amiability

We've learn the process of a handshake, so that if any part of that process is changed or interrupted, we become confused and start to wonder what we should do next. In other words, we become open to suggestions.

The process of the Handshake Interrupt gives a break to the normal process of the handshake, long enough to give a suggestion.

Handshake Interrupt Version 1

Milton Erickson's version of the Handshake Interrupt takes only an instant to do, but to explain it is rather complicated.

The handshake begins normally, by extending the hand and grasping the other person's hand. The interrupt begins just after the hands meet, and the controller then de-focuses the eyes, with a blank, expressionless and unblinking gaze. When pulling the hand away, the fingers disengage, but the thumb tightens around the upper part of the hand, while the fingers separate; then, letting go with the thumb and just before letting go, slowly tighten the last two fingers around the hand, and slowly pull it away, while gazing blankly into the eyes of the subject. At that moment, the subject will pause and freeze in a state of momentary catalepsy, in which the hand remains locked in position, and the eyes glaze slightly.

The operator must use sensory acuity to note the momentary instant of confusion that the subject experiences. At that moment, a suggestion can be given. Such suggestions can fall under the category of "feel good" suggestions, like, "Connect very deeply now," or "Relax, you will be fine" or "This meeting is important."

At that moment, the operator can create amnesia for the

suggestion, by returning to conversation and completing the handshake as normal.

Other suggestions can be given that don't fall under the "feel good" category and are more mischievous than malicious. The operator can tell the subject, "Look at the hand and stay... right there," and the subject can be left there, looking at their hand for quite some time. One operator has reported to have told the subject, "Your feet are stuck right where ... they are staying."

Handshake Interrupt Version 2

This variation of the Handshake Interrupt is much more direct and simple.

The operator initiates the handshake and, at the moment of contact, the operator de-focuses the eyes and gives a blank stare and then lifts the subject's hands up to their face, with the soft but direct command of, "Look at the hand" and holds the hand in place. What follows is often a string of commands. "Notice the distance of the hand and the depth of your thoughts, and when the time is right ... now... close the eyes and ...go inside..."

In both these versions of the Handshake Interrupt, the operator refers to the hand of the subject as "*the* hand" not "your hand." By doing this, it "disconnects" the subject's hand from the subject, and they begin to see it as something that is separate from themselves; and if it is separated in that way, it can be manipulated by an external force.

Brain Pirating

"Brain Pirating" is the name of a Mind Trick practiced by hypnotist Jeffrey Stephens, as a way of getting people's attention and promoting his own hypnosis practice.

During this Mind Trick, Stephens describes how he causes the hand of a clerk at McDonald's to hypnotically stick to the counter.

NOTE: THIS WILL NOT WORK IF THE PERSON IS BUSY!!! And that would be wrong to do, anyway, as it would be interfering with their business.

First, let me say that I am no expert. Just a guy who likes playing with hypnosis. And when I go places, I like to test my skills and give people a story to tell their friends. I also tend to draw attention (not intentionally), by the fact that I typically wear a hat. Not a 'ball cap.'

Mind Control 101

I wear either a homburg or a fedora, the latter being my favorite. And since this isn't common anymore, people tend to look at me just a little closer. I also wear sunglasses, even at night. (Adds to the mystique, you know.) They are polarized, so they don't interfere with driving or anything else.

So I will walk into, let's say Micky D's, and go to the counter. Because my sunglasses are just a little bit oversized (they are glass-lensed, polarized, fishing glasses, for those who know what I am talking about), the person behind the counter (whom I will call Tom, for no apparent reason) tends to look at my face a bit more directly/intently. (Trying to see my eyes, I would guess.)

Tom asks if he can help me (or take my order, or what ever). I quickly note something to focus on (ie. a necklace, bracelet, ring, etc. - something personal) that I can draw his attention to and get him to start focusing inward about.

So Tom asks his question. Then I say, "Yes."

Then I pause for just a moment and then say, "I would like..." [PAUSE] "Interesting necklace. I *'like' that." (Give just a second or two to allow Tom to mentally move inward.)

"...a Big Mac meal."

What I have just accomplished is the following:

1) Tom focused on me for a second or two.

2) He went into his one-line spiel, which has the effect of putting him in the 'zone'. (By this I mean that he is now listening for any of the words on the menu. He is 'expecting' to hear certain things - with just a small margin for things like "hey," "hi," "yes," etc.. Tom has been saying his 'opener' for hours and getting "Yeah, give me a number one..." over and over again. It is now what he EXPECTS (that is the key word) to happen.

3) I meet his expectation precisely. And then throw him a curve.

4) By immediately turning his attention to something that will make him mentally turn inward, I have created a pattern interrupt in his brain. This is why necklaces, chains, small medallions, etc. work best. The item is personal, but they cannot readily see it, and so they must turn inward, to get a picture of it.

5) As though in mid-sentence, I continue with my order. I have now drawn his attention back outside.

Mind Control 101

To recap (and I hope no one is getting angry that I am making this so detailed): I drew his attention to me. Then let him drop into 'zone.' Then moved him in that direction, slightly. Then completely turned him inward. Then immediately pulled him back outward, in a way that creates a slight bit of confusion, since he thinks he missed part of what I was saying, because I began speaking in mid-sentence. By this time, Tom's brain is off-balance.

Back to our show. Within a second or two, Tom is punching the keys on the register, and I jump right into a statement, such as, "Isn't it interesting how different people like different things. I like that 'necklace,' as I am sure you do, too. It's all a matter of preferences. Funny how the mind works. Different people 'stick' with different things. You get 'stuck' with the things that 'hold you down' and appeal to you." Note that I have not waited at any point for Tom to tell me anything about his necklace. Flow is everything. Tom: "Will that be all?"

"Yes." And keeping my eyes on his (though mine are behind sunglasses), I pause for about 2 seconds and say, "The mind is a strange thing, when you think about it. The way it gets 'stuck' to something and 'just can't pick it up." (I hold a $10 bill closer to me than to him.) I never look away from his face. And if he looks away from mine, I quickly do a reverse nod (ie. head flicking up rather than down), to draw his attention back up to my face (subconscious directional control, perhaps?)

Tom: "Your total is $5.47."

I hold the bill forward, very close to the counter (calm down, still a ways to go). Tom will break the 'eye contact' at this point, since he has to count the change out. Now this is the point where the whole thing can fall apart. If Tom is 'not too swift' and has trouble counting your change, or if he has to ask for change from the manager, because he has run out of quarters, or anything that completely breaks the flow (and this could be you, hesitating too long, as well]), it just isn't going to work.

On average, you will have ideal flow maybe 1 out of 5 or 6 times. But all the rest are good setup practice. So go for it. Just don't get frustrated. Enjoy the practice, and see what you can learn from it. But PLEASE NOTE that if the flow is broken, DO NOT proceed with the rest of this, as Tom will think you are a freak. And that is not what you are going for.

While Tom is counting the change, I say, "Your mind may make you do things you can't seem to explain or understand. Perhaps you 'hand' someone their change, and 'you get stuck.' (This is timed to be as he finishes counting the change and is moving his hand toward me.) My hands, both of them, are still on the counter, just about halfway between Tom and myself. Since my hands are resting lightly on the counter, and I make no move to lift them, Tom starts to lower his hand toward mine.

"Do you see it?" (This remark is intended to get Tom to look at me in the face again. Another quick reverse nod helps here.) I point toward the counter, which he sees peripherally. (Both that last remark and this gesture are sufficiently ambiguous, as to put Tom in a (very) slightly confused state.) Tom reaches to put the change on the counter near my hand. When he does (all of the following assumes that Tom is right-handed), I tap the side of his hand with my right index finger (sometimes several times, kind of like doing Morse code), and gently push downward with the first two fingers of my left hand, until his hand is touching the counter. "You find your hand is stuck, and you cannot lift it, no matter how hard you try. 'Try,' but you cannot lift it."

The look on Tom's face at this point is extremely gratifying to my playful sensibilities. I quickly pull out a business card that I have strategically placed for this quick flourish. Tap his hand (which has now only been 'stuck' for a few seconds; perhaps 3 to 4 seconds) with the card and say, "Back to normal." (Or alternatively, "You can lift it now.") As his hand comes up, I extend the card with a smile and say, "Hypnosis is a very powerful thing. 'You can take control of your life. Hypnosis can help make it happen.'" (Those last two sentences are on the bottom of my business card, as my slogan.

I smile, take my change, and step back to wait for my order. And I enjoy it, as Tom goes back and starts talking about what just happened. For weeks following this, the people watch me closely whenever I go there. And sometimes ask for my card. And by going only at times when business is very slow, I give them the chance to ask me questions.

If nothing else, you can use this technique to think about other ways you can use influence techniques within a normal situation or context.

Enchantment

Enchantment is a term that comes from magic, and in all of my personal experience, it seems to be the most powerful and positive form of Mind Control. It is positive because, in my experience, everyone wants to be enchanted (it is the opposite of being cursed), and it is powerful for the same reason.

To get the feeling of enchantment, imagine being told a story or a conversation that draws you into a magical world, where anything is possible, and you know you are completely safe to go there.

Like some of the psychic influences, enchantment requires the operator to do a certain degree of work on themselves, first. You will find that when you are able to create the mental state of enchantment as an operator, the rest is easy.

Because no one I know has done any work in the field of "influence by enchantment," what follows are my personal observations and models on the subject.

Attraction/Liking

Contrary to most models of influence, the first quality of enchantment is not the outcome but instead a love for the subject. This is not a sexual or romantic attraction but an intense liking. This means that, regardless of the established relationship between the operator and the subject, the operator feels a deep attraction to the subject. This feeling of attraction/liking causes the operator to completely focus in on the subject in a way that most everyone would enjoy. It creates a compelling feeling of attention within the subject that increases their willingness to follow the operator's suggestions.

This intense liking also compels the operator to pace the subject, making rapport very easy.

The Outcome

Once this attraction/liking is established then the outcome can be given some focus by the operator. To use an analogy, attraction/liking is the boat and its engine, the outcome is the rudder that guides the vessel.

Fulfillment

The feeling of fulfillment is the next quality. If the operator is feeling completely fulfilled with the interaction, then there is no sense of disappointment, regardless of how the subject responds. This feeling of fulfillment results in the operator having a greater sense of flexibility, so that if something does not work, it is okay, and something else is tried.

Eagerness/Excitement

With the rapport that is created through attraction/liking, the eagerness/excitement of the operator subtly creates a willingness in the subject that compels the subject to follow. This model of Enchantment is strictly my own. As you go through this process, consider how you would want to be enchanted, if the opportunity came about. Your outcome as a controller would be to create something magical and to start that magic with yourself.

You will know when you've got it, because the magic will linger.

Good luck - and I wish you something magical.

What are the Personal Dangers of Using Mind Control?

Perhaps this is obvious, perhaps not. The fact is that this may not even be a hazard, except for a few. It is the detachment from the rest of humanity. There is a fine balance one must maintain between our loving connectedness with humanity and the objectification that occurs, when you look at people as if they were sheep to be led. No one can teach this balance, and it most often occurs as a result of long, mindful meditations. It is essentially a paradox; on one end, you are human and a part of humanity, on the other end, you seek to elevate yourself and become separate.

I can give you no advice on how to deal with this paradox. Only to make you aware of it and wish you well.

But there are worse maladies that one can suffer when using Mind Control, and so I list for you what they are. If there is a sign of them in your behavior, it may already be too late.

Signs of being out of control
Egomania

Mind Control 101

If you get a taste of power and the ability to influence others there is a hazard that has befallen even the most sane people. Having influence over others will tend to make one susceptible to believing in their own self-importance and infallibility.

Paranoia

Believing you are infallible may lead one to perceive any opposition, no matter how slight, as a wholesale assault. With just a little bit of nurturing, this could escalate to reclusive behaviors and stock piling of firearms.

Signs of paranoia?

* As a general rule, it is when you start collecting weapons, for the sake of protecting your cause.
* Reclusive behavior.
* Preaching an us/them gospel.
* Talking about your enemies and how to deal with them, more than having fun.

Restricted World View

If you begin to believe in your own self-importance, it is likely that you will also begin to believe in all sorts of bullshit you are telling yourself. The detriment of this is a closed mind and loss of willingness to consider other possibilities and world views. That is like becoming the ex-smoker, who now makes a smoker's life hell.

If you start to take yourself too seriously and can't laugh at your own screw-ups (you will have a lot), it is probably too late.

Obsession

Obsession is like a drug. It keeps you up and energized, but it also restricts you in ways you can't imagine. The worst part isn't the obsession; it is when you lose interest in your obsession. Then you are likely to suffer depression and begin looking for your next fix.

Believing that your doctrine is the answer will prevent you from exploring any further.

To avoid obsession, your best remedy is to have a full life ,with many dimensions. A wide variety of friends and interests should keep you balanced.

Sadism

Mind Control has gotten a very bad name, because of the abuse that the mentally unstable can do with it. For a few, power over others creates the willingness to test the limits and leads to unrestrained abuse.

As mentioned in the beginning of this book it is best to do only those acts of Mind Control which you would want others to do to you.

Anyone who uses Mind Control will find it much more rewarding, and with more benefits to motivate your subjects, by having them want your presence instead of fear it.

How to use Mind Control and not become a paranoid, gun-collecting nut that sees conspiracy at every turn.

By far, one of the best ways to keep yourself from tipping off the deep end, while employing the tools of Mind Control, is to have a diverse group of friends, who have no fear of telling you when you are full of shit. These could be drinking buddies or just friends from your past.

A more systematic way of keeping yourself in check is done by some groups that fully understand the possible dangers of tipping off the deep end using Mind Control. They assign an "insubordinate" to every person in their hierarchy. The purpose of the insubordinate is to give unrestrained criticism, without punishment. This was the position of the court jester of the royal court.

Keep in mind, you don't have to agree with what they tell you. You only have to listen. It may be the best advise of your life.

Conclusion

What you will learn by applying Mind Control in your life

If this hasn't frightened you and you've, in fact, managed to read this far, there are only a few other things that you will experience, if you continue to study Mind Control.

* Mind Control becomes an obsession, or at least a sincere interest. It will be one of those things you will want to constantly test and master.

* It is not as important as it used to be. Once you begin to "think up a level," you will raise yourself above the turmoil, compulsions and desires, that first motivated you to learn to control the thoughts and actions of others. The result: a calmness that puts things in a clear perspective. Your original obsession with Mind Control and power will have been realized, and your next desire will be to see how skillfully you can wield that power. Ultimately, as you are surrounded by the calm that true power brings, your ambition will be to see how little effort it takes to get what you want.

* Power is a tool, nothing more. As much as we try and should try to elevate ourselves above them, the true persuaders of our actions will continue to be our fears, vanities and appetites. To believe anything else is to embrace a Pollyanna simplicity, and deny our origins as animals. Even though this is from where we've come and will continue to be a part of us, we should attempt to raise ourselves. Though it is a futile effort, it is a worthy one and it's an attempt to grow.

There will always be a vast majority who continue to only allow these impulses to guide them. Ultimately, your goal is to not be one of them.

Mind Control 101

Recommended Mind Control Movies

* The Usual Suspects
* The Grifters
* Runaway Jury
* The Sting
* Scanner Darkly
* The Trueman Show
* The Sixth Sense
* Unbreakable
* Signs
* 1984
* Dark City
* The Matrix
* The Mothman Prophecies
* The Manchurian Candidate
* The Butterfly Effect
* The MTV cartoon 'The Maxx'
* The Power (old sci-fi horror movie about super psychics bending reality and perception)
* Silence of the Lambs
* Red Dragon
* V for Vendetta
* The Illusionist

Additional Resources

The 33 Strategies by Robert Greene

The Art of Seduction by Robert Green

The 48 Laws of Power by Robert Greene

Perfect Mind Control by Dantalion Jones

Gaslighting, The Double Whammy, Interrogation, and Other Methods of Covert Control in Psychotherapy and Analysis by Theo L. Dorpat

Don't Shoot the Dog by Ellen Prior

Deeper Insights Into the Illuminati Formula by Fritz Springmeier & Cisco Wheeler

Combating Cult Mind Control by Stephen Hassan

1984 by George Orwell

Forbidden Keys of Persuasion by Blair Warren

Never be Lied to Again by David Lieberman

How to Get Anyone to do Anything by David Lieberman

Enchanted Evening by Kenton Knepper

The Frame Game: Persuasion Excellence by Michael Hall

An Insider's Guide to Submodalities by William MacDonald and Richard Bandler

Any religious of the hundred of religious texts that are used as doctrine.

Printed in Great Britain
by Amazon.co.uk, Ltd.,
Marston Gate.